LIZ CAILE:
A Life at Treeline

Columns by Liz Caile

Edited by Claudia Putnam, Kate Readio and Kay Turnbaugh

Perigo Press

Published by: Perigo Press, KLT Communications, Inc.,
PO Box 99, Nederland, CO 80466, 303-258-7075

This Perigo Press volume is the first book edition of a collection of newspaper columns by Liz Caile which were originally published by The Mountain-Ear over a span of 20 years.

ISBN 0-9702532-0-6

Library of Congress Card Number: 00-191473

Cover design by Kay Turnbaugh
Cover photo of the Indian Peaks by Bill Ikler
Photos courtesy of Ralph 'Skip' Greene and Barbara Lawlor
Map by George Blevins

Text printed on recycled paper. A portion of the proceeds from sales of this book will be returned to the environment.

I want my stories to come from places and
things I know in nature...I want to take some
of my craziness and bury it ritually in the right
place in the earth, to find a cure for my restlessness
in plants and planets, roots and rituals. I want to
strengthen my life choices—conceived through
intuition—with stories about things that are mine
from living amongst them and watching them.

—*Liz Caile, December 24, 1992*

Thanks to:
Liz's Family
Lee Tillotson
Bill Ikler
Cece and Steve Miller
Nature's Own
The Mountain-Ear

LIZ CAILE: *A Life at Treeline*

Treeline (or timberline):
The altitude beyond which trees do not grow.

Contents

SIMPLE LIVING

3   First winter: in on the ground floor

5   Free to think the wildest thoughts

7   Wind system works because we think small

9   The Forest and the Sierra Club cup

11   Economy and the economy

13   Simply a few observations

15   Stuff: last of confessional illness

17   Lessons to be learned from the English

19   Does a car really mean freedom?

21   One man's pimple house, another's palace

23   A home should fit a hillside

25   Spend money at home for a sustainable economy

27   A real letter is the rightful occupant

29   You hear what you want to hear

31   One learns by small increments

33   Living with limits is good science

35   A marriage of respect, not convenience

37   Early people at eye level with nature

39   They came to die, but they found life

41   Long-time residents: 'profoundly located'

43   Sourdough kicks off the New Year

45   Their lifestyle makes the endangered list

47   Navajo lifestyle holds a message for the future

49   Telling stories like a native

51   An intentional lesson from Earth

LIZ CAILE: *A Life at Treeline*

Contents

THE SEASONS

57 And I would be connected...
59 Earth like a newborn's skin
61 Escape to world of lichens
63 Extra hour turns into day of appreciation
65 Thanks for water, willows and geese
67 Ripening cones: late summer harvest
69 Shrinking inventories and opportunities
71 Butterflies: what better way to speak of love?
73 Has there ever been such a sky?
75 Grassy Top cures the blues
77 Silent Night: Variations on a theme
79 Skiing comes on like a sneeze
81 Solstice is a time for telling stories
83 Winter sends a dual message
85 Searching out the winter blues
87 Water miracles in our backyards
89 This lively circle of spring is testimony

ENVIRONMENTAL ETHICS

95 Politics is the answer, as well as prayer
97 Growth is like a piebald cow
99 Attitudes about land change slowly
101 Trouble with a capital P
103 Perplexed by paving mania
105 Mountain bikers, hear my quarrel!
107 Bring native landscapes into mind
109 Shoppers are reshaping the world
111 A nation that just says yes
113 What are your terms of rebellion?
115 Time to turn the corner on true conservatism

LIZ CAILE: *A Life at Treeline*

Contents

117 Watershed thinking changes the world
119 Don't abandon Earth for space
121 The darker it gets, the faster we drive
123 Life forms signing off the web
125 Forest Service could save time, money by protecting web of life
127 The mystery of the disappearing toad
129 No turning away from dying land
131 Reforming business and industry
133 'Resourcism' has got to go
135 Salmon is more than a slab in the store
137 Shall there be strip malls in Belize?
139 Open your mind to creative housing
141 Talking to Earth is like talking to one's children

SOCIAL VALUES
147 On Indian claims to art and ceremony
149 Bring on the (medicinal) pot
151 Suppose we listed the cause of death?
153 Socialization has holes in it
155 When the killing has to stop
157 Sacred geography touches all
159 Let's not silence ourselves
161 Irritating words create a pearl of truth
163 We take 'The News' as served

WAR & PEACE
169 The questioning has gone on and on
171 Belittling observation misses the point
173 We're building shelters for <u>what?</u>
175 What then is for us?
177 Post-war celebrations miss points

LIZ CAILE: *A Life at Treeline*

Contents

AT TREELINE

183 Unlock the secret for reverence for land
185 Not all trails are good (or bad)
187 Boulder Canyon: a gorgeous drive
189 Colorado bicycling in the 1940s
191 Mountain search had its price
193 Small home design takes years
195 Bird count helps define ecosystems
197 Jets destroy Braille of simple sounds
199 Brainard can't take any more blacktop
201 Outages cause outrage, but think again
203 Avalanches happen in the real world

FAMILY

209 She told her stories and inspired others
211 Families suffer from delamination
213 Thanks for the view, Dad!
215 Keeping my son on a tight rope
217 Lessons learned away from home
219 Remembering another graduation
221 She skinny dipped in the ocean of light
223 Belated Mother's Day greetings
225 With Boo on my back
227 Grandmas and superheros

WALKING

233 Walking nurtures an open mind
235 Mountains are sometimes victims
237 Discovering the surface of the land
239 Give gift of walking shoes
241 Walking has been the nicest thing

FOREWORD

What does it mean to live an authentic life?

Words spring to mind: truth, integrity, courage.

Liz Caile believed in living lightly on the earth, in using our resources carefully and thoughtfully. She believed in being conscious of the impacts of our actions, as a nation and as individuals.

Liz wrote a column for *The Mountain-Ear* for 20 years. *The Mountain-Ear* is a weekly newspaper published in Nederland, Colorado, a town of 1,700 in the Front Range of the Rocky Mountains. Its closest neighbor to the east is Boulder, and to the west it's the Continental Divide. Liz began working at the paper when her two youngest sons were starting school. Often the three of them walked to town from their home on Sugarloaf, several miles away. Liz read to the boys as they walked and talked. They lived without modern conveniences in a small cabin with their dog Girly, and Liz reveled in their life. She felt strongly that this was the best way to bring up children—close to the natural world, close to the written word, and close to each other.

When the U.S. Forest Service bulldozed her cabin* because it was on an unpatented mining claim, she took up her pen, writing about her experience and warning others that destruction of similar cabins

---

*In 1897 National Forest land became available to miners, who could prospect and extract minerals and eventually file a patent on the land, buying it for the price of a government survey and $1.25 an acre. Patented mining claims are private property, but if a mining claim is unpatented, except for mineral rights, it still belongs to the government. Some of the cabins that remain on public lands were built during the boom years of the West's mining towns, some were built later during the Depression years when the U.S. government encouraged people to build a place and mine the ground under it. In the late 1970s, many of the old log cabins on unpatented mining claims were demolished by the U.S. Forest Service. The Service said that residence in cabins on unpatented mining claims was trespassing, even if the resident bought the cabin, unless it was actively connected with a profitable mine. The Service also thought that the cabins were often unsightly—surrounded by old hardware, auto parts and junk cars, and that the buildings presented a psychological encroachment on the public domain. A picnic bench now sits on the site of Liz's cabin.

around the state was a threat to our history. From those words, others started to flow, and a regular column was born.

Liz's writing for *The Mountain-Ear* tended towards the environmental, and as time went on, the political. She was one of the first reporters in the world to cover (or uncover) the acid rain phenomenon. She pushed and prodded readers in her columns, wanting everyone to see the world as a symbiotic whole the way she did. She never wrote down to her readers, in fact, she was probably one of the most literate writers working for newspapers today, making readers look up her words, making them think about the relationships, the causes and effects she observed.

She wrote a book of poetry, and she put together a personalized, anecdotal cookbook. She reviewed books for *The Bloomsbury Review,* and she wrote about the natural world for many other publications. Her journals from the last ten years of her life filled the trunk of an American car.

Liz and her husband Skip incorporated their values in their everyday lives, using alternative energy and conserving resources. In her columns for *The Mountain-Ear,* she reminded us of the true costs of growth, of consumerism, of paving, of war, of too many signs on the mountain highways, and even of our footsteps.

A true child of the '60s, for Liz the personal was political, and she worked to balance the contradictions inherent in modern life. She walked when other people would have driven. She railed against low-flying jets streaking across our skies as they leave Denver International Airport, but she relished her chances to travel, to places like New Mexico, Costa Rica and southern Colorado. She lived most of her life without a telephone, but when that modern convenience came to her home, she enjoyed the contact it provided with her friends and family, especially her three sons, Billy, Ben and Dan. She worried out loud, walking the hall at *The Mountain-Ear,* searching for ways to weave what she wanted to do into the fabric of her principles, struggling to make peace with her ideals by bringing them to life in her columns.

Liz lived an unconventional life that was full of integrity. She avoided the current prescriptive definitions of family values and success. Liz lived and loved in her own heartfelt and thoughtful way.

As an active member of the Mountain Forum for Peace, she learned the techniques of mediation, and often she offered her services during hot summer afternoons in *The Mountain-Ear* office. Her desk was up front, where she could greet visitors, something she liked to do when she was stuck while writing her column. Writing a column on a weekly basis is a tough thing to do, and for Liz it was often like childbirth, a painful but joyous process. It's something she did astonishingly well, and won awards for, in spite of her weekly worries.

Her columns frequently made people angry—and she worried about that too—but that's what her kind of column writing is all about. Years after she wrote them, people remembered her columns. They remembered the ideas she wrote about because of her lush and poignant imagery.

Liz was 53 when she died on Valentine's Day in 1998.

For a couple of years she had been fighting what the doctors told her was rheumatoid arthritis. It was a brain tumor. As the cancer, which she still thought was arthritis, spread and made her life more painful, she continued to write, and some of her most inspirational, beautiful columns were written between visits to doctors and hospitals, waiting for test results and visiting with friends.

She left a void, and we miss her unique intelligence and perspective. But her writing remains. Bringing this book together has been tremendously gratifying for us. To read her finest columns as part of a single collection is to walk beside Liz again, and be reminded of the gentle persistence of her point of view and her eloquence in expressing it. Once we had the pieces in one place, we saw that Liz had given us, quite simply, an awe-inspiring body of work.

We will always remember Liz as a devoted mother and grandmother, wife and daughter. As a community and environmental activist. But most of all, we remember Liz for her writing—for her graceful descriptions of our beautiful places. And for her work to save those beautiful places for all of us to enjoy.

Kay Turnbaugh, Claudia Putnam and Kate Readio
February 14, 2000

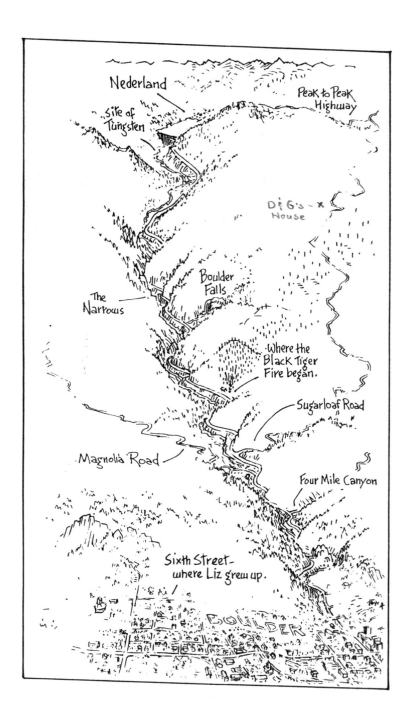

SIMPLE LIVING

*Liz and her husband Skip at their house
near Ward, Colorado.*

A Life *at* Treeline:

SIMPLE LIVING

*I moved to the mountains from town life with
some impossibly idealistic notions about what
was supposed to happen: notions about self-
sufficiency and a more wholesome way of life,
notions about letting the environment cure the
anger and tensions of modern life. I put high
hopes on the hands-on therapy of wood and
water and fragrant masses of dough...we
turned our backs on comfort and conformity
not just for the pleasures of the simple life, but
in a true search for meaning.*

—August 1994

I drank sunrises for breakfast and sawed wood outside by lamplight in soft falling snow.

First winter: in on the ground floor

I n November 1970 the cold settled in about the same time I moved into a mining cabin on Sugarloaf Road. The cabin was filled with old furniture, with supplies left from miners who had bunked there temporarily, and with a leaning stash of drywall and bits of insulation still to go up. I found boxes of rat poison in the drawers and didn't understand yet that the cabin was a magnet for woodrats.

I didn't bring much to my first mountain winter, except a craving to be off the beaten path and close to the land. I brought my five-year-old son and our possessions packed into the cubbies of a VW bus. I bought a bow saw, mittens for both of us, two new turtlenecks for the kid, a set of thin cotton long johns. We had J.R.R. Tolkein's *Hobbit* and *Lord of the Rings* books, and the army-surplus five-gallon water can that had been part of my divorce settlement after five years of marriage.

I was determined to live in the mountains; the fewer conveniences the better. I had a dream about it comprising a better life; I had a hunger to be close to land with continuity. Upper Sugarloaf then provided a continuous blanket of natural country, home to native plants and animals, and a connection to the past of pioneers and of Native Americans. We were miles from the nearest neighbor.

I learned about hauling water from a spring, gleaning firewood from the surrounding pine forest and aspen groves, bow-sawing the thin trunks, building fires in the pot-belly, filling kerosene lamps and trimming their wicks. I learned without serious catastrophe, though the drainpipe from the kitchen sink to the outside hillside froze, and I burned the sleeve of my parka by setting the lamp below where it was hanging.

I began to see things in new dimensions. As water from the springs above the cabin created a broad ice flow, I started parking the car by the road after work, sometimes carrying my sleeping son up the silent hill. A full moon hung over our little clearing. For the first time I was stunningly aware of it as a sphere, a vibrant satellite, much more than a face. Dropping little Billy on the couch, I'd crouch to start a fire, scrunching up paper, adding dry aspen fingers, then building a confined teepee with thin logs. I learned to set the drafts and dampers.

Billy would wake up, rub his eyes and kneel next to the fire with his drawing pad on an upholstered hassock. He would draw his mountains, dragons and hobbit holes, while I cooked dinner on a small propane stove in the kitchen, marveling that butter wouldn't melt in my cold hands. Eventually, the outside propane tank was exhausted. A friend procured a handsome wood cookstove for me. I knocked out the wall between the tiny kitchen and small living room—deconstructionism at its best.

I have a doctor who keeps throwing drugs at whatever is crippling me now, proclaiming I live in the mountains, I must be there to get out and do things, so I've got to try it all. But I didn't move to the mountains to do things, so much as to take in mountains on their own terms. Waking in the morning with no switches to hit for heat or light, living above the earth by inches (no foundation, no insulation or finished floor) was like waking up on the ground floor of life. I could hear the mountain spirit breathing outside the door. It overpowered our fear of Tolkein's shadowy Black Riders as we huddled together reading each night.

I snap-trapped the woodrat and discovered its beautiful coat, I lost one dog and went around with blackened fingernails and soot on my cuffs. I ironed my little boy's sheets with a hot cast-iron frying pan each night. I drank sunrises for breakfast and sawed wood outside by lamplight in soft falling snow. I learned that survival was sometimes a simple matter of waiting out the storm.

—October 9, 1997

Free to think the wildest thoughts

I was looking over old journals and I realized that not so long ago, though it seems like eons, a loaf of bread in the house was a luxury item for me and my two kids. I was living on the edge, on less money than some people spend on beer and cigarettes. But I was raising the kids where I wanted to be, where I could give them skiing and ice skating, bicycling and running, hiking and nature study right out the front door. This was my idea of freedom.

Besides that, I was on hand to play concentration, baseball or to read to them most any time of day. We were a little short on furniture, so we played concentration on the floor. I couldn't believe I could get down to that level—but once I got there I discovered the game generated a certain amount of neural firing in the brain.

I thought freedom was living without a flush toilet. Running water and electricity cost money, which demanded a slavery to a job that paid just enough to break even on the rent, food, car and day care. Work didn't bother me, I don't think—each day I put in hours cutting wood with a handsaw and carrying water in a bucket or pail—what bothered me was that I couldn't make choices about the worthiness of my work if I was going to live in the high-rent bracket. Somewhere along the line, I got this idea that you

5

should live what you do and believe in what you do. Work should serve humanity and not detract from quality of life on the planet.

Freedom, too, was living without a car. So my kids learned to walk, a skill that will be one of the most valuable things I taught them. You can always get from here to there on your own two feet.

So what did we eat if we didn't buy bread? Mush—the infamous mush—from grains ground in a hand grinder and boiled in spring water; tortillas—they don't squish when you put them in a pack; homemade bread and biscuits; pancakes; eggs, cheese; tofu. Some of it was pretty disgusting, but nobody got scurvy.

And we were free to think the wildest thoughts and watch the wildest sunsets. Free to believe in a world where the best things in life are free.

—February 7, 1991

*We have a
lot of quiet
time, when
there are
no electric
motors
running
within a
mile or two
of us...*

Wind system works because we think small

I have received a long letter from a reader who questioned some of my ideas and augmented his opinions with a friendly description of his own experiences. I get the feeling that our opinions would mix about as well as oil and water, while both of us have loved to walk the old railroad route through our mountains.

He questions whether I ever got anywhere with wind power, expressing skepticism that this alternative technology would work.

He's not alone in his skepticism. Just a few weeks ago, we had a government expert on wind and solar power in our home. He wore an offended expression the whole time he was there. He seemed not to want to hear us say that our wind system was adequate for our needs. He may even have felt we were traitors to the American tradition of excessive consumption. From his place inside the government bureaucracy, he assured us that wind power just didn't cut it, and that photo-voltaic panels were "black art" (a really forward-looking guy!).

In fact our wind system—initiated and maintained by my husband—works because we think small. We have used it for most of our electrical needs as long as I have lived at our home, twelve years, and it was working for others some time before that. We do use gas generators for some tasks, once or twice a week. We don't have a refrigerator. (Who needs one, I always ask, at 9,400 feet in the Rocky Mountains?)

We have a lot of quiet time, when there are no electric motors running within a mile or two of us (though the highway roar is ever-increasing). We have a lot of satisfying times when the wind generator is running at a steady hum. On dark winter mornings when it's running like that, I turn three lights on at once, for the luxury of it, as well as to "load" the batteries, which is supposed to be good for them when they are charging. When the machine is producing power, it sounds like a busy bee, something like blue-grass music. Our small wind generator, with a seven-foot rotor, on a sixty-foot tower, has been designed to survive the killer winds around here that have nullified more than one wind-power dream.

We put a fair amount of time into monitoring and maintaining our system. We use two large deep-cycle marine batteries to store power to use when the wind is not driving the generator. We have a small TV, a tape deck, and a lot of light fixtures that date back to original designs for "sky lab" systems to run off solar energy. We charge small recyclable batteries for other appliances from the wind.

And yes, I can write a column with wind power, and quite a bit more, on the computer we've added to our system. With the computer, we added an inverter so that we can use DC or AC power at the flip of a switch. We also invested in an efficient battery charger, so occasionally we can boost our batteries with the gas generator.

How you judge this system depends on where you are coming from. If you've lived without electricity and with kerosene lights, you feel rich for not having the fumes in the house and having enough light to act like you live in the twentieth century (at times, a dubious achievement).

What we have is a somewhat eccentric system that teaches us about engineering systems and how much energy we really need. It relies more on human energy and ingenuity than fossil fuels, once it's been installed. You can judge it as you will—by an arbitrary standard that assumes there should be no limit on consumption, or by a yardstick that gives points for conservation. Take your pick.

—August 26, 1993

The Forest and the Sierra Club cup

My father loves to tell about the good old days and the way you used your Sierra Club cup when you were camped in the outback planning your ascent on a granite peak.

As he talks, I can visualize his fingers priming a small, reluctant gas stove and stirring something in a light aluminum pot: "First, you ate your freeze-dried gunk in it. Then, you followed with a cup of soup or hot Jell-o. And then, of course, you drank your tea, swishing around anything that was still floating in the cup so that when you were done, your cup was clean." His eyes are bright with the promise of the next day's climb.

The Sierra Club cup is a broad-rimmed steel cup with a wire handle, shaped somewhere between a cup and a bowl. We used to tie them to the outside of our packs and take them off to drink out of clear-running mountain streams. They facilitated a long, satisfying draught, as opposed to the cold gulps you'd get lying down on your stomach, face to the stream. It may be dangerous anathema to talk about drinking out of streams these days. That was before giardia was spread so profusely into mountain watersheds by dogs and other creatures.

Dad's use of the Sierra Club cup represents a sort of ideal to me, even when I am in the kitchen cooking. Let's face it, the fewer dishes you dirty, the fewer you have to wash. It represents an economy of utensils that I wish we all could take into our lives. It says some basic

9

things about our habit of consumption, drawing a line between what we really need and what is superfluous.

I've often been grateful for the perspective of camping out for long stretches of time in my childhood and for the kind of conservatism it has imposed on me. Nonetheless, my life is a never-ending battle against careless resource use, and every so often I am caught red-handed with a paper cup in my hand, a piece of forest brought down for my use, one of billions of packaging conveniences that erode our appreciation of a natural economy.

"It is important that we all understand the connection between patterns of consumption and patterns of environmental change," writes forest activist John McInnis of the Western Canada Wilderness Committee. McInnis is fighting for the integrity of Canadian forests, or more correctly, for the fragments of forest that are left. He describes the heavy pulpwood use of Albertan forests, places I once visited, though I can't recall using a Sierra Club cup in them.

Canada is part of a global belt of boreal forests that is being brokered to corporations that make good money out of turning forests into paper cups and other handy, single-use products. Heavy logging is planned for the forests of interior Alaska. Russian forests are falling both to corporations and the predations of acid rain. Scandinavian forests have become predictable plantations, while fires take their toll across Canada, a country whose government has only just begun to tune into the ecological importance of its greatest resource.

The connection between paper cups and forest clearcuts is so direct it hurts, putting the effects of careless consumption in perspective. It's so simple—and so complicated. Almost everyone of us is tied by our jobs to consumptive routines, and I can't plead innocent when you're reading me on newsprint. But we have to start somewhere.

These days, instead of a Sierra Club cup there's the ubiquitous plastic cup that easily fits in the day pack, shoulder bag, glove compartment or back seat of the car or office drawer.

Use it.

—September 22, 1994

*"Stingy,
frugal,
tight,
compulsive,
cheap,
conservative,
parsimonious
(sounds like
a vegetable—
I could make
soup from
it?)...*

Economy and the economy

I'd like to say some things about economy and the economy. They aren't the same thing, really, are they? Economy, in my book, is a practice of making the most of the least amount of resources. The economy seems to run on the principle of always needing more.

I think I've been suffering a sense of alienation from my society on account of the difference between these two things. The majority pays lip service to environmental concerns, but both the right and the necessity to make a buck seem to be, in truth, the bottom line. Meanwhile, I congratulate myself on all the economies I practice, then wonder if there isn't something wrong with me.

I spend my days rinsing out plastic bags and hanging them up to dry around the house, taking them down and folding them neatly to make order, using them for the next day's sandwiches or wrapping up a loaf of homemade bread. I never buy sandwich bags. Well, I bought a package of zip lock bags once for a student who needed them for Deb Eads' science class. Two years later I still have half the box. The last time, and only time in ten years, I've bought aluminum foil was also for a science project. Yes, Neo's, I wash out the aluminum foil you wrap left-over pizza in and use it again.

I wonder about my tendencies to scrimp and save, to write rough drafts in pencil instead of ink, in the belief that the looping lines possibly will cost me less. I even make choices regarding which sheets of scrap paper to use for different kinds of writing.

You may be reacting to these confessions with a variety of words. The words to describe my behavior seem to have positive or negative connotations, which parallel the reasons I refine and reduce consumption as I do:

"Stingy, frugal, tight, compulsive, cheap, conservative, parsimonious (sounds like a vegetable—I could make soup from it?) picayune, petty, measured, rationed, minutely discerning, quantifying, hoarding, holding onto meager resources." On the one hand I weigh my choices from fear and selfishness. I fear being drained away to nothing, being stripped of power, or of the freedom to pursue my own interests and needs.

On the other hand, I conserve resources because I love the land. I don't want to see the natural world used up. I feel hypersensitive to the loss of living, wild, beautiful things I've observed in my own lifetime, from people gobbling up resources or simply plowing ahead with the human habits of comfort and conformity. The county I have lived in all my life except for the first three years has added significant amounts of pavement and pollution every year.

The beauty of the wild things that have been lost or endangered was something you could swim in. What is left after wilderness has been tamed and appropriated is, instead, a wading pool. Up to the ankles in what is left, we shrug—it's better than nothing and we still have room to grow. Better than nothing, but only just.

—February 1, 1990

What, I wonder, has much of our society got against observation?

Simply a few 'observations'

One of the things I've enjoyed this summer is the endless opportunity to observe natural phenomena in action. I've had a little sun-porch garden growing and see there as well as outdoors the great transformation that takes place in a few months from seed to fruit. I walk around our yard thinking, "Grow, darn it! Rain, darn it!" focusing on all the inputs that seem to accomplish this transformation, and this mental concentration seems to get results.

There is hardly a disappointing moment as I go about with my eyes and ears open; there is always an interesting bird or bird sound, a new little insect that I swear I have never seen before. Glimpsed from the back of a motorcycle, I found two brilliantly colored wood lilies sticking up above a highway cut—flowers that I consider unusually beautiful and rare for our immediate surroundings.

Being an observer is such a marvelous pastime. For one thing, it's free. For another, it's intellectually stimulating and emotionally non-toxic. I recently was gratified to catch something going wrong with my car by applying the habit of observation and as a result avoided a costly repair.

What, I wonder, has much of our society got against observation? As I watch people driving up and down the canyon oblivious to the fascinating natural phenomena around them, with their cars falling apart behind

13

them (haven't you observed this behavior once or twice?), it seems to me that our society breeds a disdain for observation, and indifference to, or positive avoidance of, understanding cause and effect.

I don't know why this is, except that if everyone were to discover the pleasures of just looking at things and listening to things, they'd probably stop spending money at breakneck speeds—they might even stop working at certain jobs that, when closely observed, appear to be counterproductive to a healthy society.

My theories might be a long shot, but some of my observations about behavior nation-wide are shared by friends and notables. Addressing the graduating class at Bloomsburg University in Pennsylvania this spring, the great naturalist Roger Tory Peterson said: "Many people go through life as though they are wearing blinders or are sleep-walking. Their eyes are open, yet they see nothing of their wild associates on this planet. Their ears, attuned to motor cars and traffic, seldom catch the music of nature—the singing of birds, frogs or crickets—or the wind. These people are biologically illiterate—environmentally illiterate—yet they may fancy themselves well informed, perhaps sophisticated."

That's one of the problems, of course, is how we fancy ourselves. Almost every magazine we pick up, every radio station or TV station we listen to, spends a good portion of our time proposing how we should fancy ourselves—in Wranglers, smoking Marlboros or Virginia Slims, up to date with an Apple or an IBM...We have, perhaps, gotten out of the habit of looking at how we really are and what we really need, to the point that to look closely and objectively at the natural world or even at the structures of our society upsets our sense of security.

I'm not talking about an "environmental issue," unless you define your household and personal lives as being as much a part of the environment as clean streams and how many rare and beautiful plants are surviving in the county. I simply propose that observation is a skill that enriches life at all points of contact, and one that is worth cultivating.

—*July 12, 1985*

14

Stuff manage- ment is an art and a science, and just possibly a wellness trip.

Stuff: last of a confessional illness

A lot of companies advertise "stuff" as a premium. I think it's a disease. Like alcoholism or cancer a decade or two ago, no one likes to talk about it. Keep it in the closet!—if only it'd stay in the closet!—if only the closet weren't packed to the gills!

When I read about a woman who was competing in a race across the Atlantic Ocean by rowboat and who said she did it to get down to the basics, I heaved a sigh of understanding. How much stuff can you worry about in a rowboat mid-Atlantic besides a life jacket? I thought of the view from the rowboat: the distant, constant horizon of water all around me—what a relief and what a reprieve from dealing with the overwhelming occurrence of stuff in my life that needs to be unloaded.

Friends of mine recently confessed to having made several "virtual" moves, trying to initiate a weeding process, and still they have too much. My problem is that I cannot bear to throw out things that still have a shred of use to them, and at the same time, I don't like to give time and energy to things I am not using in order to delegate them to the Salvation Army or other appropriate receptor.

One frustrating subset of "stuff" is magazines that have accumulated over the years—old *New Yorkers,* for example. Hidden in the pages of those slowly decomposing piles are some awe-inspiring short stories I may never cross paths with again. But, I want those magazines out of my house. *Natural History* magazines have pictures and articles that are still worthwhile. Boulder

Public Library no longer puts out old magazines for its readers to pick up free; Gilpin County Library has declared a moratorium on donations. Books and magazines are painfully heavy to move in any number, and nowadays, few places for recycling knowledge exist. We're on a mad course printing new versions of it.

We've reached the saturation point with our stuff, and we're still in denial. Our exploitation of many products, from cars to computers, exhausts only a fraction of their substance. Stuff, like radioactive matter, seems to have a "half-life" in which it is used and valued (blushing with pride at its possession), and then a longer amount of time in which to roam the world purposelessly or glutting the landfill.

If stuff is a disease, it occurs in forms from mild to catastrophic. Some of us can't keep our desks or kitchen counters uncluttered. Others have houses and yards that are mazes built of old cars or cardboard boxes or simply piles of stuff that they haven't figured out how or when to unload.

Stuff is potentiality, and we hate to give it away: that old car that could be fixed up for a profit; that antique computer that still works like a gem; half full cans of paint that could finish a job tomorrow; sporting equipment that waits for its moment of opportunity. Sheds, shops, closets, garages hold the physical remains of what we imagined we could do or be.

Stuff management is an art and a science, and just possibly a wellness trip. Some succeed, others fail, some drown and others gag, permanently depressed by stuff they can't get rid of, blocking their view of a clear horizon, rearing up in stubborn opposition to new and freer paths. Stuff is an outgrowth of post-war, 1950s propaganda about the good life, the ingenuousness of science and the march of Progress. Now we're stuck with it. Only the most powerful can clean up the tin-cans clinging to their wagging tails. Only the most powerful will can resist the urges heaped upon us to accumulate more stuff. Each offer entices us to buy the ultimate gadget that is going to make our lives work.

Maybe if we call it like it is—stuff as disease—we'll manage to break free.

—*October 16, 1997*

16

Americans feel threatened by the concept of submitting individuality to a nebulous greater good.

Lessons to be learned from the English

A close friend of mine has spent several months living in England. She amuses me by writing about the austerities she's observed in enthusiastic terms most travelers would lavish on the Crown Jewels. "You'd love it here!" she insists, and proceeds to outline the discomforts of living with less.

"...many women ride bikes or push prams to the shops on rainy (rain, not drizzle) mornings...a friend told me that she had to walk, not bike, her son the two miles to school because her friend had borrowed her bike seat for the day (no thought of just going out and buying one as in the States)...the house we're in would be considered impossible for a family with three children in America, yet here it's average to large. Cars, ovens, footpaths—everything is so much smaller and thus uses fewer resources."

In her letters my friend compares many aspects of English life to American: "People's expectations are high—one simply wouldn't put out dirty milk bottles, and children just don't yell or talk back...You speak less and think more before you talk. Or write. Things are very civilized. Proper. The opposite of the 'up front' qualities of the U.S. And I keep wondering which way is better. Wonder if the lack of 'freedom of spirit' would be revolting after a while? Yet it's that freedom that has led to ugliness at home, hasn't it? The often careless use of language, sloppy and cheap buildings and city planning, gross materialism and common lack of contact with any 'higher' cultural life..."

In a recent letter she concludes: "Here people live

on a smaller scale simply because of the economy. It seems to me it's an American challenge to do this for moral reasons—not because we're forced to do so. That's what influences others the most, don't you think?"

Living with less for moral reasons isn't popular in the U.S. these days. Americans feel threatened by the concept of submitting individuality to a nebulous greater good. Any many believe it's an unrealistic goal. They take the Machiavellian view that "The wish to acquire is in truth very natural and common, and men always acquire when they can; and for this they will be praised, not blamed."

Machiavelli, that Renaissance cynic, believed men are naturally wicked and the imposition of religion is the only way to overcome their baseness. Unfortunately the church in Italy at that time wallowed in material excesses and did his theories no good. Today, one has only to listen to certain TV evangelists or Indian swamis promoting material well-being to realize it is unpopular advocating the use of less, even from the pulpit.

We might consider, however, Alexis de Tocqueville's 19th century perception that "the mores of America were the foundation of its free republic." Democracy is a function of nebulous ideals. And, it is childish to think that our "up frontness" will be compromised by free-will frugality.

My friend's letter reminds me that our wealth is too often devoted to conspicuous consumption instead of to travel to other parts of the world where we might learn to define "needs" and "luxuries" differently. Many of our children have rooms full of comforts, but have never experienced a different culture making do with less but reaping many satisfactions.

My correspondent has found the English love of flowers and literature to be a rewarding aspect of that society. And as a mother she appreciates the emphasis on polite children! "People are more contained and used to governing their movements, to being quieter, making life pleasant within a confined space."

I think we could benefit from this sense of containment in our lifestyles even while being surrounded by wilderness. Our immediate environment would be more pleasing. And on a global scale, our lives would be secure with the knowledge that we are trimming our resource use to fit what the rest of the world already takes for granted.

—July 26, 1985

Oddly enough, I have had the strongest sensations of freedom when I have been on foot...

Does a car really mean freedom?

When I got a reliable car after years of having to do without my own wheels, I heard over and over again, "That gives you a lot of freedom, doesn't it?"

Yes and no. It gives me the freedom to be somewhere besides home without spending the whole day getting there and back. It gives me the freedom to visit friends too long unseen; it also gives me the freedom to plan my shopping days haphazardly, to join the mainstream flow of little cubicles streaming down the canyon and along the mountain and flatland roads.

It gives me the freedom to take a class or teach a class, to volunteer, to chauffeur...to do any number of things with the hours I used to spend walking and sticking my thumb out to get from one place to another.

But having a car doesn't begin, really, to fulfill my idea of freedom. Oddly enough, I have had the strongest sensations of freedom when I have been on foot, and usually after I have been on foot for several hours, having gone through all sorts of tiredness and impatience to reach a state of sheer appreciation for the silent road, the near and distant peaks, the color of the sky and rising moon, the feel of the air.

Now that's freedom—an awareness that "excess baggage" has been dumped and that on my own two feet I am relatively safe and secure, within walking distance of home where I can look forward to enough to eat and the good company of my family.

One of the strongest images I have from Tolstoy's epic *War and Peace* is the description of Pierre Bazhukov's stint as a captive of the French army outside Moscow. It is, I suppose, the romantic freedom of deprivation—but his deep, internal sense of peace at having gotten down to the very basics has lived in my mind in the decades since I read this book. I looked up this episode today and read, "All Pierre's daydreams now turned on the time when he would be free. Yet subsequently, and for the rest of his life, he thought and spoke with enthusiasm of that month of captivity, of those irrecoverable, strong, joyful sensations, and chiefly of the complete peace of mind and inner freedom which he experienced only during those weeks."

My TV yoga teacher, Lilias Folan, recently remarked on freedom: "Our first notion of freedom is only the tip of the iceberg" and "Freedom lies in knowing the difference between the desired and the reality."

Too often I'm chasing the desired rather than savoring the reality when I get into my car, and that's a grudge I have against it. I wonder if it isn't one of the pitfalls of our munificent society that there is so much to desire, so much to reach for, that our real freedom is pinched and cramped by the wanting.

—*January 11, 1985*

My question is, why hasn't the example of the past been more closely followed in mountain building?

One man's pimple house, another's palace

I f you discuss politics in a crowd, ordinarily you will only offend half of your listeners or at most two-thirds. But if you want to offend everyone, you need only take up the subject of architecture, loudly, in an opinionated sort of way. For one man's pimple house is another man's palace; one woman's shack is another's Shangri-La.

If you don't know what a pimple house is, chances are you are living in one. A pimple house, terminology courtesy of an old friend, is one of those houses that sits in the middle of a beautiful meadow, has an eroding driveway cut gracelessly into it, erupts an ugly two stories into the air and confounds the eye with half-modern, half-traditional planes of glass and varnished wood.

I am partial to the shack—the one-story dwelling protected from the elements by faded tar paper that reminds me of lichen on rocks or tree trunks. It seems to back into the hillside from shyness, and is protected by an old pine or spruce tree that towers above it. Or it nestles birdlike behind a screen of aspen. It's so low, by today's standards, you'd think it was inhabited by midgets—and it probably would never pass code.

There are, as far as I'm concerned, a vast number of buildings imposed on the mountain landscape that should never have been built. They are eyesores. They don't belong here.

Consider a hypothetical example culled from the real estate section of the classifieds: "The essence of New England in this mountain home—30 minutes from Boulder." There happens to be several thousand miles separating us from New England, and many cultural and environmental differences as well. I have the same reservations about the Spanish hacienda style in the mountains as I do about Cape Code classics. Then there are the generic subdivision types that seem to belong somewhere else, or what I call the "hippie teutonic" style—impressive castles of rough-hewn, beetle-killed wood that look terribly hard to heat and years away from being finished.

Have I offended everyone? My question is, why hasn't the example of the past been more closely followed in mountain building? Some of the surviving, original log cabins fit into sites that naturally catch the warmth of the high altitude sunshine and naturally avoid the worst of the winds.

In the mountain towns the most attractive homes are often old frame houses that fit on small lots. They fit, in part, because they are small and, in part, because of the simple but refined use of planed wood. Even larger buildings can be made to fit into the mountain setting if built without a confusion of phony angles or the imposition of vast windowless walls.

Examples of mountain architecture that I appreciate include the Presbyterian Church in Nederland—simple but well proportioned, the old church in Ward, and some of the new passive solar homes that have cropped up, both sensible and sensitive to their setting.

We all have to live somewhere—and there's no accounting for individual taste, but building in the mountains too often appears to be an act of stamping possession on the land without demonstrating respect or understanding. Mountain living should be more of a marriage with the land than most contemporary building suggests.

—February 15, 1985

The ideal home is accessed by paths and separated in some way from cars...so that coming and going our feet can remind us of the nature of the land...

A *home should fit a hillside*

When forests are running out of trees and brown clouds creep and brawl out of single valleys to take over whole regions, resources are at a premium. No wonder over-large homes are labeled irresponsible and to some, morally offensive. But what makes a good home? I have several ideas. To begin with, I think a home should foster a connection with the land and the community. It should bring the community into contact with elements of nature, so we'll know what needs our care.

Not so many years ago the location of a source of water and how a family would access it was the first step in planning a new home. Now water is taken from town utilities or with great feats of technology so that we can maintain only a consumer's relationship to the substance. A friend of mine, who had to drill deep to meet the county's requirements for water, nonetheless practices collecting rain water, heating water with passive solar, and using and reusing water in a variety of ways. Doing so, he maintains what could be called a sacred relationship with water.

A home should fit a hillside. I can think of two models for this fit. In one, the home nestles into the south-facing slope, minimizing the obtrusiveness of its geometric lines and its exotic materials on the landscape and taking full advantage of the insulation of earth (or tires and earth) walls and the heat sump of its foundation. In another model, the foundation consists of poured concrete pillars—the house rises from the natural contour of the land without gouging out a piece to force a platform.

I like space for myself, and I like small, small houses, too. The search for the happy medium in home size could, perhaps, make new use of the modular home concept. We could add rooms for growing children or home business activities and subtract spaces when they were no longer needed. Our space needs fluctuate widely with the stages of our lives.

Windows, I think, should light one's indoor life. I've just read that light from two sides of room, as opposed to only one, is beneficial. Views are important to feed the soul, not the ego—it's probably big enough already. I love to step inside the small mining cabins I come across in my wanderings, with light pouring in from unintended openings, to see what was framed by the original builders. I marvel at the intimacy with wild grasses and shrubs, or the view to receding foothills, or the small window to the west—a foot square—that opens like a prayer on a distant peak.

One aspect of homes I've lived in for over two decades has contributed greatly to my thoughts and happiness. I've had to walk to get to them. The ideal home is accessed by paths and separated in some way from cars, I think, so that coming and going our feet can remind us of the nature of the land and our eyes have time to find the sky and learn its language—and connect us to our neighbors.

The homes I am fond of require a certain amount of physical energy from their occupants: walking to them, moving water around to heat or conserve, shoveling walks, sweeping floors, tending to maintenance chores rather than mailing off utility payments. Such homes are a revolt against wastefulness, against exploitation and most of all, against boredom, because our ingenuity is once again engaged where it matters most—in our homes and neighborhoods, on the land.

—*April 28, 1994*

Spend money at home for a sustainable community

I like to imagine the holidays in the mountains twenty, fifty or 100 years ago, to go back and feel the way winter and long nights possessed the land. Some years would be mild and open, and the water in the shallow creeks would wave up at the sky; others, the storms would stream in and hold the pines and grasses in a cold embrace, the water would stutter and freeze in its tracks.

The people living in the mountains in small settlements would find gifts for one another in their pantries, and perhaps, through a few exceptional mail-order purchases. They'd use their hands to craft quilts and wooden boxes, forged tools and accessories. I can imagine the potluck dinners and dances, inside the community hall or school house: the old men's fingers running over piano keys and mandolin strings, curiously alive of their own accord, independent of the old faces, the bodies shaped by daily work; the rhythm of feet hitting the wooden floor like pegs, a fine, fast repetitiveness to the dancing.

Outside, the dry grasses knee deep in the valleys, unless crushed by a cycle of snows and winds and drifts, would exhale the smell of stems and paper thin strips of leaves into the cold dry air of the valley, frost pasted across the thatch of meadows, the dark pine trees at the edges nothing more than shapes like animal fur at midnight with no moon; the sounds would rock the valley, and afterwards, the land would become quiet and only a natural light, broken by the occasional candle or kerosene lantern would intrude.

Is this nostalgic picture sheer indulgence? We're taught to believe that nostalgia is. Everywhere we turn to find solutions to living on the planet peacefully, we're discouraged by loud voices telling us to conform to the current "realities." In contrast to the miners who lived here fifty years ago, say, and walked as much as a dozen miles each day to work and back, earning a very modest slice of the pie, we've got no backbone—we believe the persuaders on TV and on the radio waves who tell us that being American means going into debt, flaunting waste and modelling extravagance. And yet, closer to home, in a straight line back in time, we can see at least one other way.

Pigeon-holing nostalgia is one way of blinding people to place and their own priorities. In another instance of put-down, a preacher who admonished his flock to spend less for Christmas and avoid going into debt was attacked for acting like "Scrooge." What seems like appropriate advice from the pulpit, coinciding with the impoverished but meaningful birth in the manger, became a target of criticism from Rush Limbaugh, who stands for nothing if not the American way of self-serving politics. Limbaugh wants the reverend's flock to continue in a debt-slavery to the CEOs who make millions, even billions—the men and women who live inside walled compounds and build houses big enough to hold half the forest at Christmas time.

We who are so fortunate to celebrate the holidays in the embrace of living pine trees can also celebrate our community and the idea of a sustainable community, by shopping at home and by staying out of debt. We do several things, by making holiday giving conform to community and our own budgets rather than to the grandious expectations fed by the mind-benders who grow rich from our complacent folly. We save transportation miles and expenditures; we strengthen our local businesses; we stay within earshot of the creek; we have more time to make our own cards, knit our own gifts, cook our own cookies, and still get rest, so when the time comes, we can dance all night and still have energy for the morning chores.

—*December 14, 1995*

26

You cannot be a tightwad when you write a letter.

A *real letter is the rightful occupant*

Have you ever wanted to return to some real—or imagined—time of innocence, when the only things you ever found in your mailbox were really and truly addressed to you? When even the occasional bill or library overdue notice had specific information in it that was yours alone? Then, the empty mailbox had a clean, clear message to tell: your friends who owed you letters were derelict in their duty.

These days you are more likely to empty your box day after day of wads of slick advertisements and so-called personalized messages and to feel guilty—given such quantities of mail—to be disappointed that there are not letters addressed in a unique and individual script.

Junk mail reminds me of trash fish, or of exotic species introduced to an ecosystem whose members take off in a reproductive wildfire and crowd out what is supposed to be there. The demise of letter writing as an art and pastime can be blamed on many causes. Overlooked is the intimidating stream of classy, printed, glossy and decorated advertisements and solicitations that come our way familiarly embossed with our name and address, in the possession of a promiscuous computer.

But a letter written by hand is the real thing, the original and rightful occupant of the mailbox. Whether scratched out in a hurry, rambling around the margins of a greeting card, or thoughtfully composed on reams of paper, a real letter has a quality that I treasure and have been trying to define for some time.

I have been searching for words to describe that quality especially since last summer, when struck by an organization virus, I went through fourteen years of letters and cards with an idea of straightening out the mess of their informal collection.

The organizational surge was drowned out by strong currents from the past. I spent hours gripped by one of the most moving experiences I'd had in months, re-reading those old letters.

Almost without exception, an incredible honesty and straightforwardness goes with the handwritten letter. Though years and miles had almost obliterated a friendship, an old acquaintance's core personality would jump out at me from a casual written communication I had saved. I could picture not only the face but the hopes and dreams, likes and dislikes of that person. I could also feel the strong will for friendship and connection in each and every letter I had saved.

A genuine generosity goes hand in hand with the written word. You cannot be a tightwad when you write a letter. Writing is an act of sharing that has no equal among all our other acts of communication.

In Paul Scott's Raj Quartet of novels, his strongest character, Barbie, is a letter writer. At the beginning of *Towers of Silence* she explains:

"I know that my own addiction to pen and paper is a form of indulgence. It's also a form of praise, I mean praise for the fascination and diversity of life which if you notice it yourself is always nice to bring to someone else's attention. I have written eight letters, which means that there are now eight people who know things they didn't know, for instance, how beautiful Pankot is and that I have hopes of living here."

Barbie, a perfect fool in some respects, believed in sharing her thoughts in writing, a gift that was often ignored by its recipients. Too bad. Today it would be more welcome, as the personal letter in a sea of computerized junk stands out—like a jewel in a tinseled crown.

—May 29, 1986

Sound is a diagnostic tool for our equipment and for our surroundings.

You hear what you want to hear

This paper has a saying, "You hear what you want to hear, and you see what you want to see." What does that mean, some people ask, that there's no grounded truth? To me it's akin to "judge not that ye be not judged"—a reminder to look more closely at your relationship with the rest of the world.

You walk by a town meeting and see a group of people in discussion in there, and you don't hear—you don't want to hear—any of it, although the discussion is at times about things that will affect your life. If you're there, you'll probably selectively edit what makes sense to you, based on prior prejudices.

Sometimes I want to bring natural sounds into meeting rooms to expand what's being heard—like bird song from the wetlands and shrublands that are dealt with so summarily. The varied songs of different sparrows, found in different tiers of mountain wild lands, are incredibly soothing. They bring me a unique sanity, a calmness and faith, though the small birds themselves are seldom seen.

Sound is a diagnostic tool for our equipment and for our surroundings. Imagine: a chickadee that warbles; a raven's caw deep and honking; a sapsucker's nest that sounds like a squeaky distributor shaft (seems like the similes are all backwards these days); shimmering aspen like distant tambourines; the creek in the distance sounding like a wind beginning to comb the ridge; tiny impacts on wood—a woodpecker scuffling on a trunk or a chickaree, turning a cone in his hands, pulling off the scales with his teeth.

You see what you want to see, and you hear what you want to hear. Highways offer the ineffable delights of varied tire noise—tires out of balance and misaligned, tires ill-designed, the rumbling of Harley pipes oddly exempt from legal decibel limits; the irritating bleep of back-up signals. I'm glad I have a choice in my day.

I love the library of information all my senses bring to me, individually and combined, each sense and behavior intertwined with the world: the thump of a deer's hooves as it wheels away—a muted percussion that alerts me to the animal, horns in velvet, who slows to look back; the sound of a car dropping off a friend at the bottom of the road; the school bus telling time on a winter's morning, distant on the highway; the shine of tools, a familiar footfall, a swelling of evening wind, the welcome nattering of rain.

Insect sounds change with the season. In the midst of extreme dryness, when fire danger rattles my bones, I listen to an interminable chirruping coming from the woods. At least someone is having fun!

And other sounds: pans bumping against each other from a hanging rack, a sleeper's breathing, the morning fire—or the terror of flames crackling high inside a chimney; stiff bristles against the floor sweeping. The roar of a river, the flood of an electronic band, water running where it shouldn't be; a biplane, a jet or the eerie air-rip noise of a sail plane. Distant thunder, a snipe whistling high overhead, voices raised, the irritating rounds of ammunition being spent.

Sometimes I think we have less choice about what we want to hear than about what we want to see. Man-made sensations often overwhelm the natural. But the world we perceive is, to a large extent, our own creation. You hear what you want to hear, and you see what you want to see.

—June 30, 1994

I want to know if a life-time of pathological aversion to convenience makes sense.

One learns by small increments

You know how it is: the first time the temperature drops seriously below freezing, and suddenly, you're standing with your butt to the woodstove, thinking all that matters is the fire within it. Well, maybe you don't know, but it's a familiar scenario for me, and I'm giving it some thought, especially since two of my friends have declared, "this year we're switching to gas!"

The subject is convenience, and the price we pay. Either way, it seems, we pay a price.

I look back fondly on coming to the mountains to live in a small cabin, without utilities. It became a sort of catch-phrase—"without utilities"—two words to convey a choice to be in touch with the elements on a daily basis. I think about the boots I owned then, a pair of Steve Komito's duty hiking boots. The then-Boulder boot maker would pick one practical, affordable style and stock it in bins. They were a single ply leather that softly fit my foot and had a Vibram sole, and I wish I could will them back into existence. They gave me my first serious lesson in leather care: they fell apart completely after one or two years of wood-gathering in them and drying them in the oven of the wood stove—don't!

I look back on my years in the mountains when I'm trying to figure out how I could end up with the kind of arthritis I've been experiencing. I always believed that if you use it, you won't lose it, but that ain't necessarily so. Now, when my wrists scream in pain, I look

31

back and see them in constant motion: hauling water in an old army can, dragging wood out of the woods, cutting it with a bow saw, daily. Feeding the stove, emptying the ashes, lifting the black cast iron plates with a handle that fit so neatly into a recess.

I started living alone in a small cabin in the fall. The stove was my mantra, still is. It's a centering being. It heaves and sighs and creaks and billows. It radiates heat. The closer you are, the cozier it is. It is convincingly alive. I am looking at it, wishing it could talk. Can we have a conversation? "Is this worth it?" I want to ask. I want to know, if a life-time of pathological aversion to convenience makes sense.

But cast iron is a channel for other spirits. It speaks for the wind, it speaks for the tree that grew on the hill. It speaks for warming and cooling, and boiling water on top. And that's what I love about it. I love knowing things, little things going on around me. I love the silent conversation of the woods, and how, in the fall, the dead trees start to show themselves among the green, and I begin to evaluate whether they are ripe for the stove or if they have another cause to serve: bird house, bird perch or even lattice-work to hold soil on the hill, to turn in time into a gray-green bed of lichen, a patch of brilliant moss.

How can you evaluate time spent outdoors not going any-where, just creating little paths to dead wood, graduating into time spent helping with the wood—side-lined, willingly, by the chain-saw, buying into that convenience, at least. I have one explanation: one learns by small increments about the woods, the quality of heat, the sound of unpredictable combustion, the nip of cold as the heat dies down. One way to learn the environment is to depend on it, instead of on energy inputs from far away.

I can't guarantee any special returns for this knowledge. And, there is a time to move on to new knowledge. Still, for me there's pleasure in looking back, remembering the way aspen falls to the bow saw, the first roast turkey coming out of that old black stove, and the way we ringed the stove: dogs, children, and I, at various times, inside a warm cocoon, surrounded by a thick quilt of fairy ice, floating as if on a small sloop in the middle of an awesome foothills ocean.

—*October 3, 1996*

Living with limits is good science

An experiment in living with limits has arrived at one terminus, as eight people have left a 3.18-acre sealed environment in Arizona. Most of us have heard of Biosphere 2; many are aware of a taint of skepticism that has accompanied the earth-ship, space-colony simulation.

Some scientists challenged the quality of scientific experiments planned for the sealed space. Now, at least one of the original skeptics endorses the endeavor, and many others are impressed by the accomplishments of eight people living in harmony with each other within a limited environment.

They grew their own food, ground their own wheat, mended their own clothes and lived with serious oxygen depletion for a period of time, gamely carrying out their two-year mission to explore the interactions of soil and water, sun and air within a closed system. When they debarked, each provided the press with a list of foods they had craved but couldn't have. By most accounts, none of those foods would actually make them as happy as the two-year experiment did—and, it lowered their cholesterol.

While some of their methodology may be questioned, the Biosphere crew has demonstrated that rather than creating misery, their necessarily frugal lifestyles promoted happiness. Their lives were in direct contrast with most of ours, where we are always being persuaded there are no limits. Charge it! Switch it ON!

Refinance! Whatever it is you want, you can find a way to have it—this is the marketing plan of the twentieth century: a consumer population that never says no.

Meanwhile, all the information we have points to limits to the planet as an important, though chronically ignored, fact of life. For example, studies from nearby Niwot Ridge show that the atmosphere's capacity to carry away pollutants is limited. Atmospheric nitrogen that forms acid compounds is up 30 percent from levels measured a few decades ago at the tundra biosphere research site.

Biosphere 2 scientists exited two years of confinement in a simulated closed system with remarkable *esprit de corps*. This in itself is good science, a confirmation of an old truth that man thrives on cooperation when limits are imposed. They modeled the experience of many tribal societies, whose customs are shaped by limits and include extraordinary respect for all members. In this sense, they reconciled modern science with ancient tradition.

If you don't know what suffices, you can never be satisfied (Lao Tzu said that, more or less). This serves the marketplace, but not the planet and leaves us quite confused about what is really needed and what is really us. When Biosphere 2 botanist Linda Leigh said, "I have glimpsed paradise," I translate it to mean, working with the limits of her environment, she knew what was real, and the sense of it was bliss.

Imagine those eight people standing together and drawing a circle of such a radius to create an area of 3.18 acres, working to provide for much of their needs within that circle. Now, imagine your home or community as the center of a similar circle. Make it as large as a county or a major watershed, but call a limit and see if you can sustain the resources for yourselves, others and future generations within that circle.

—September 30, 1993

Mechanical things run best for those who fully understand them, and that under-standing takes both time and passion.

A *marriage of respect, not convenience*

Contempt for the machine is cheap and easy for those of us who are oh-so-environmentally correct. We can't avoid machines in our lives, so we act out our contempt by treating machines poorly or simply ignoring them, as if mentally to say, "you can't rule me." It's a mistaken relationship—and in its wastefulness, destructive of the natural resources we profess to love.

Sierra magazine recently asked readers, "If you could de-invent one machine, which one would it be and why?" Some answers that strike a chord with me include the bulldozer, the photocopier, "any motorized contraption in the kitchen," and "the horrible leaf-blower," which stirs up all kinds of dust, dirt, droppings, exhales carbon dioxide and ruins the sound environment. The infernal—oops, internal—combustion engine takes a hit, air-conditioning, cars and snowmobiles. Notice no one mentioned the vacuum cleaner or the washing machine!

Swami Paramanda Sarasvati, from Nederland, gets right to the round, smooth, constantly-in-motion heart of things and de-invents the wheel. No wheel, no snowmobile, whose track runs on little, round hard plastic gizmos—and that inspires me to want to change the direction of this discussion, because I benefit from snowmobile access to my home. While many mountain residents are cutting hillsides in half to access their homes and churning up good earth plowing off every snowflake, I walk clean and easy on snowmobile pack.

The earth below the snow, my feet, stays put together as it was by nature in the first place.

I've learned a lot from living with these little machines, which are hated as if they were the devil incarnate by skiers who probably think it's their god-given right to jet back and forth over my house and the Wilderness for every opportunity that comes their way.

What I've learned from the snowmobiles that haul my heavy loads up the hill and from their proprietor, my partner, is that machines function most cleanly when they are treated with respect. I've also learned another curious and difficult lesson: if we are to live with machinery at all, we—or some of us—must give them the same rapturous attention we give to other aspects of our lives. We are married by circumstance and by temperament to the **mechanical arts**, and any art takes practice. Only an impoverished philosophy allows us to think machines are servants that we can pick up and dispose of at whim, or monsters who necessarily rule us.

I, too, have imagined living without machines. I clean with a broom, wash some clothes by hand, walk instead of drive when possible, wield a shovel to clean the water bars in our minimalist driveway. I crave a world of living silence instead of the annihilations of motor and engine sounds. And I admit, it stretches the mind to consider, along with which machines to discard, the ultimate, machine-less world.

A more promising course, however, is to envision a marriage between the machine and the primitive selves we are protecting at our core, a marriage of respect and not convenience. Mechanical things run best for those who fully understand them, and that understanding takes both time and passion. (If we don't fully understand the machines we use, the least we can do is to exercise compassion.) Combining our physical and mental resources as human beings, with an appropriate homage to the mechanical arts—as in "small is beautiful" and "appropriate technology"—could go far to resolve contemporary environmental problems.

We need to appreciate that part of ourselves that invented machinery in the first place and get on with the task of lessening our impact on the natural world.

—December 14, 1995

Imagine a curtain that has been opened, not on a stage explained by scientific theory, but on a universe of infinite depth.

Early people at eye level with nature

I have been reading Jim Benedict's work on the pre-historic inhabitants of our mountains. Benedict has studied alpine and sub-alpine evidence of their presence, which he dates as far back as 5,800 years. Imagine for an instant the intensity of their world.

He describes the seasonal movements of the people up and down the valleys and river courses and over passes; he postulates a yearly, counterclockwise migration of Indian bands from, roughly speaking, the Boulder area, north along the foothills, over the Divide, south through North and Middle Parks and back towards the plains by way of local passes. I feel beauty most keenly when he describes the gentle hog-back region, and also, the last summer campsites in the ecozone between tundra and forest. I sense a foreign beauty to the rocks he describes as tool material—foreign to my mind which has never studied geology; beautiful as another facet of the landscape etched into the pre-modern mind.

How do we grasp the experience of the people at eye-level with nature? I'm interested in the consciousness behind the evidence of stone tools, spear points and scrapers, bits of pottery impressed with patterns of twine, above-timberline drive walls and cairns, sub-alpine hearths.

What gets to me is the extrapolated realm of their knowledge, from the awareness and observance of tiny insects, mosses and flowers, to the nighttime presence of stars, planets, moon, clouds and northern lights. Was their awareness of the change from day to night different from ours? Imagine a curtain that has been opened, not on a stage explained by scientific theory, but on a universe of infinite depth. Did beauty and terror combine in every moment of existence?

Where and how did they sleep? Did they suffer as we would suffer if we tried to imitate them? What comforts, what joys (ah, the hot springs!)? What picture could I paint of their migration routes becoming suddenly clogged by a pale reflection of themselves, men who fastened to one spot, accumulated fantastic geegaws and began to devour land and trees and game, but never moved on?

Two details of Benedict's papers struck me particularly. Before the twentieth century, great herds of elk and deer and bison migrated in and out of the parks. But the newly arrived white men, with their guns and appetites, and the competing Indian bands, who had appetites too, decimated the herds. Decades later the animals made a "comeback" in the parks—the herds growing from a few remaining individuals into a plague of ruminants, but without that old ancestral memory of sinuous, meaningful movement over the land. What have we done, I ask compulsively.

The restless bands of Indians traveling across the Divide on their way back to the mild, sandstone-walled valleys, discarded their worn grinding stones near its crest. They left enough sandstone in this form to momentarily confuse the white man's categorical mind. Some early geologists speculated the Rocky Mountains must have pushed up through a continuous layer of the sedimentary rock, so numerous were their abandoned artifacts—tools that looked like rocks.

Visiting with us, Benedict served up another morsel: he suggested that the Indians placed clear chert arrowheads into the water at Hot Sulphur Springs, where in a week or two the stone points would turn opaque—whitened in a way that is similar to weathering that takes a thousand years. He has found reworked pieces of stone that exhibit patinated layers that could not have been achieved by time alone, and he imagines that the Indians put the stones in the geothermal waters as an offering, a dedication, and in return received a signal transformation by the gods.

—March 28, 1991

They came to die, but they found life

One doesn't have to dabble for long in the history of Boulder County and its mountains before discovering that while some people came here to mine or to ranch, some as wives and mothers, some as teachers or preachers, there was a goodly number of men and women who came here to die.

One such immigrant was James Walker, whose homestead on the backside of Flagstaff mountain is preserved as open space and a memorial to the past. His story was given in abbreviated form in a recent article in the *Boulder Daily Camera:*

"[He was] a Virginia farmer who was dying of yellow fever when he came to Colorado in 1869. The young man's last wish was to meet Indians and breathe the sweet cool Rocky Mountain air before he died. He lived with Arapahoes west of Boulder for a time, regained his health and eventually settled on the Walker Ranch."

Not long ago I talked to a woman who is a Boulder native and whose father also came here expecting death. He came from New York with the doctor's warning that he had just five years to live. He met his future wife in Evergreen, where she played organ for church. The couple waited five years before marrying and starting a family to make reasonably sure he would be around to care for them.

Two aspects of these stories impress me. The first is

that this place should have been chosen by those faced with suspected terminal illness. Leaving behind the security and comforts of the city and settled society, they traveled to the frontier, to the edge of civilization. They chose the colors of nature over the brightness of city lights, the simple life over the sophisticated.

And many found that what they had come to enjoy in their dying moments became their healing balm. They chose to return to the garden of nature to mitigate death's cruelty. Living, they must have gained a deep knowledge of what is satisfying in life.

This is the second aspect of the recurring story in local history that impresses me, though it is, admittedly, more conjecture than documented fact. Having found that natural beauty healed as well as satisfied a dying wish, these settlers may have contributed something substantial to an evolving, mountain-oriented way of life—the knowledge of what is enough.

When we try to pin down what we admire about life in this portion of the mountains fifty, sixty or more years ago, it may be something derived from the experience of those who came to die but stayed to start families and work homesteads. It was, perhaps, a combined acceptance and appreciation of finite quantities in nature.

In contrast, our search today for life's meaning is hampered by a way of life that emphasizes limitless quantities—of gasoline, of water, of grocery store goods, of new products, even of personal energy. If we believe in limiting the use of material resources, we are called doubting Thomases. It is a secular heresy to espouse a doctrine of limits. "Attitude," we are told, will overcome all obstacles as we are prodded to rally 'round a way of life based on unlimited growth.

It's interesting to wonder what a James Walker would make of all this—or of the brown air he would see from the top of Flagstaff on the wagon road where he made infrequent trips to the plains. I imagine he would conclude that it's darned hard to place a value on anything, when there are supposed to be no limits.

—November 7, 1985

The words suggest a state of grace that is absent from many of our lives.

Long-time residents: 'profoundly located'

Not long ago I came across an expression that seemed to apply to some of the things I try to write. In a long, descriptive article on a French farmer, I read, "In Europe there are still people who are profoundly located." In part, that means that when a Frenchman speaks of love of France, he is speaking literally of "the vines, the soil, the trees."

Profoundly located. The words suggest a state of grace that is absent from many of our lives. However, I am reminded of this phrase when I listen to oral history tapes of members of the Sugarloaf mountain community, tapes recorded by John Graham and S.K. Levin around 1976.

Many of the folks who committed their voices and recollections to this series of tapes have since died, having been born in the first decades of this century to some of the earliest settlers in western Boulder County. Ernie Betasso is unabashedly my favorite speaker. His voice, still so alive with the satisfaction of a life well-lived in one place, inspires great affection. I also have a physical image of this good-natured man, a miner and rancher and city parks benefactor, formed in gratitude for the rides he gave me when I was hitching to and from my old home on Sugarloaf.

Maude Waggoner is another clear voice that speaks for the sense of being located, as she recalls the stories of her birth on Sugarloaf and the charming occasion of a dance in Wall Street— "Of course, you had to do your chores before you could go." And going meant walking several precipitous miles, dancing all night and walking home, accompanied by her grandmother as chaperone.

Mining, dancing, schooling, ranching, walking, courting, riding, hauling—these are the recollections the Sugarloaf old timers put to tape, and to each activity there is a place on the hillside, a road up the canyon or a trail between gulches, a potato patch, a spring or a homestead cabin, engraved in the speaker's heart and mind.

All of their lives are recalled with fondness but not without respect, even awe, for the work and determination that were necessary ingredients of the early years. Imagine, for example, canning a few months' supply of butchered "beef" over a wood stove. "Being Italians we ate a hell of a lot of spaghetti," said Betasso, "and there were many meatless days," but his mother's canning preserved meat when it was available.

A forceful note is sounded when the old timers talk about their new and young neighbors. They welcome them, they appreciate a shared loved place, but they are confused by their near-hostility to one another—forming cliques and wanting to close the door behind them.

Says one woman, "You didn't just invite a few people in, everyone was invited. Everybody liked everyone else—there was never any of those clannish cliques that they have here now—this one won't talk to that one and somebody else won't talk to somebody else. Fiddlesticks! If they'd learn to live by the code of the hills, they'd be a lot better off. That meant you'd treat everybody just the same as you'd like to be treated. That was the way it always was...

"You'd be in trouble, you'd get a knock on the door. Open the door and nobody'd be there..." But there would be a bag of groceries sitting on the step.

These old friends and neighbors might not represent centuries of living in one place on the land, as the "profoundly located" of Europe do. But in the personal recollections they share with us, our long-time local residents suggest that there is a strength that comes with being "located" that may be of value to all of us.

—May 10, 1985

It is also a symbol for continuity and, ultimately, mystery.

Sourdough kicks off the New Year

I intend to kick off the New Year with what I fondly think of as "Ms. Hudi's" sourdough starter. That is, I'll serve pancakes on New Year's morning, 1988, whipped up from the sponge I started on New Year's Eve, 1987.

Some people, obsessed by genealogy, proudly claim their sourdough starter goes back to a gold rush camp in the Yukon. My starter hasn't such longevity, but can be traced back in a direct line through dozens of beginnings of bread doughs and pancake batters to the home economics room of Mrs. Peggie Hudiburg at Nederland Junior Senior High School.

There, quartz-crazed middle schoolers reconstructed mining era commerce in the spring of '87. Sourdough starter became a home room industry, and I had the right connections to come by a portion of it for myself.

Sourdough pancakes have a uniquely satisfying taste, and anyone who has ever eaten them knows you just can't flip them off the stove fast enough to satisfy an average crowd. Sourdough itself symbolizes many virtues with which I'd like to start the year. For starters, it's something that's always there and just needs a little bit of coaxing to turn it into real food. It's a defense against economic setbacks, hard times; it's a symbol of frugality.

Then, it fulfills certain conservationist tendencies in me. Sourdough starter, a silky cup of batter teaming with live yeasties, requires no disposable packaging or fossil fuel refrigeration. It hangs out at the ready in any relatively cool spot, and if you can't find one of those, you can just use it more often to keep it lively.

It's remarkably cold hardy too. My starter has survived freezing temperatures more than one night so far this winter. Even though this batch has been started from domestic yeast without the stamina we associate with "sourdoughs," I suspect it's incorporated some wild strains of yeast into its pedigree along the way. As a variation on the something for nothing theme, the yeasts that create a sourdough starter can actually be gathered from the air, lured into a bowl by a bit of flour and potato water set out on an open window's sill.

Sourdough is a symbol for renewal. After you start a sourdough sponge, mixing the starter with warm water and flour and leaving it overnight to rise, you take a cup of this revitalized mixture out for the next batch before using the sponge for any number of things. I have recipes for breads—molasses, steamed and corn, for bannocks and biscuits, cobblers and cakes, cookies and muffins, waffles and more.

It is also a symbol for continuity and, ultimately, mystery. Someone out there might know all the secrets of how yeast multiplies and leavens bread. I don't, and that is half the fun of it—the magic of its action and fragrance.

Finally, as one cookbook tells me, "measurements are not precise." Well, that's a blessing. Guess I'll add a little buckwheat flour to New Year's morning's pancakes and set the table with jam and molasses. What a way to start the year!

—*December 31, 1987*

44

The Black
Tiger fire
swept
through the
Sugarloaf
area just
north and
east of
Nederland
in 1989,
taking with
it 44 homes
and other
structures.

Their lifestyle makes the endangered list

 Have you ever built a house with your own hands, out of the materials that Nature left lying around? Everyone should have that experience once. It is the most satisfying experience I know...and it has made us the tightest little society in all the West."
—from Wallace Stegner's *Angle of Repose.*

I think this experience, of building a house by hand, out of the materials that nature or a too affluent society left lying around, was one of the things that created the celebrated sense of community that was Sugarloaf before the Black Tiger fire.

Many of the homes lost to fire were a sort of alchemist's miracle, something spun out of nothing much, like gold out of straw, or crafted from the woods of long ago. They were homes that had gained a sort of organic status on the mountain or that seemed not to have been built on it but to have grown from it. When fire, like a panther, swept up the gulches full of timber and moving summer air, ripping and clawing at human abodes, these it devoured most completely, spitting out only a layer of black ash.

Black Tiger took more than memories and destroyed more than could be rebuilt, no matter how generous the donations, how full the coverage of some insurance policies.

In contemporary lingo, what was threatened has now been moved to the endangered list. A lifestyle that was pushed to the edges of existence by county government rules is now that much closer to extinction, at least in Front Range counties.

What is lost, missed only after the first shock waves have passed, is the quality of sunlight or moonlight pouring in through an old log cabin's window, or the precious sound of the wind uninterrupted by the hum of the refrigerator, or the freshness of grass on a summer morning at daybreak when one first steps outside to take care of morning business.

Black Tiger took the dens of pack rats and revisionists, of those who reach back to a simple, self-sufficient past on the hillside, evading to the best of their ability both county codes and contemporary cop-outs.

Tacked at the end of one of a dozen stories about the fire are Paul Balbin's remarks. They contain the only mention of these critical losses. Paul's remarks were subtly, perhaps unintentionally, discredited by the reporter, who documented them as "claims" instead of affirmations:

"Paul Balben (sic), claiming to represent 'the viewpoint of the lunatic fringe,' asked the building inspectors if structures must be rebuilt in compliance with 1988 county codes.

" 'We don't want conforming structures,' Balben said, claiming that he did not need electricity or plumbing. 'We are not interested in an enormous expense to maintain our lifestyles.' "

Speaking for 'the lunatic fringe,' Balbin was attempting to put a name to endangered species status. For me, he points out the losses. Concludes the story in the *Daily Camera:* "Rob Helmick of County Land Use did not encourage Balben. Adjustments could be made to the building code, but would be reviewed by a special board." You bet.

Lost are the historic cabins, the small homes and eccentric palaces that had evolved as some pioneer's vision of a world that used less, instead of more. The future probably will be biased in favor of bigger, better, newer, more energy-dependent homes; the small, the less convenient, the old, the self-sufficient, carried away in the tiger's jaws.

—July 20, 1989

No loose ends, no knots to cut, no wasted remnants of wool.

Navajo lifestyle holds message for the future

The beauty and powerful art of Navajo rugs derive from the weaver's perception of the integrity of the landscape. The meeting of land and sky, the repetitive yet changing patterns of buttes and bluffs, of interspersed bush and of wind-rippled sand and rock are inspiration for the geometric patterns and relatively simple color schemes of the old rugs that have become invaluable to collectors and public treasures exhibited in museums.

This perception belongs to a people who have lived closely on the land. Today, as these people are forced off the land, either because of the Congressional mandate reached in the Navajo-Hopi joint use area, or because of their own tribe's agreement to exploit their land for its cash value in leases to energy and mineral companies, or because of the federal government's use of land for strip mines and uranium mines, waste storage or the like, this perception becomes part of an endangered way of life.

Just as endangered species of plants and animals have unique adaptations to their environments so that their genetic make-up is invaluable and irreplaceable and perhaps desperately needed in some future time, so varied ways of life within the human population may hold keys to the future that we don't appreciate or blindly fail to preserve.

Writing about the weaving process as practiced by a Navajo family living a semi-nomadic life on the land in the 1930s, Gladys Reichardt, author of *Spider Woman,* explained that the Navajos don't use cutting instruments as part of their weaving. Tapered ends of wool are overlain in the weft. The warp is connected to the loom in such a way that all of it is used up and tightly incorporated into the rug. No loose ends, no knots to cut, no wasted remnants of wool. Much of Navajo life on the land is based on using every portion of the resource needed and provided by the land, the sheep, and the closed circle of water falling from the sky and collecting dependably only in certain places.

The colors of wool they use in weaving are drawn up from the land, from the salts of the earth and roots and leaves of plants. Plants are recognized as individuals and harvested accordingly— what a bizarre and foreign notion to our way of life—and beauty is as much an entity to be treasured as money and other possessions.

Should we ask ourselves if there is something of value, something that we need to save from this way of life? Should we place a high priority on preserving it in a viable form, not just in mothballs in exhibitions?

It seems to me that to save endangered ways of life among the human species as well as in plant and animal communities, on the assumption that they may have some presently uncomprehended value to us, we have got to relate energy issues to each and every potential extinction.

The Navajo can serve as a model in many ways that makes mutually assured survival a natural extension of our lives and not a crimped, controlled exercise in self-denial. If we can incorporate lessons about waste and train ourselves in a perception of beauty that is independent of possession or consumption, more endangered species will have a chance of living.

—December 12, 1985

Venus as bright as a search light; the swan stars pointing west; the Pleiades pale beside a blaring full moon...

Telling stories like a native

Gary Paul Nabhan's *The Desert Smells Like Rain* is a pleasing book with short chapters describing Papago Indian life in the Sonoran desert. Though the desert seems distant from our mountain reality, the lessons he shares are one and the same with those we must learn about our near environment. Nature's way of doing things turns out to be best; people should adapt to nature, rather than the other way around.

Nabhan talks of how the Papago people possess the land through their intimate knowledge of it—regardless of official deed. He conveys their familial relationships to plants and animals and even land forms. He explains some aspects of desert ecology that most of us would miss in our cursory examination. While our initial reaction to these phenomena might be skepticism, the soundness of Papago practices have been scientifically documented.

Nabhan explains that a pelting, ephemeral, natural rain storm germinates many more wildflower seeds in the desert than an artificial spray of an equal amount of water. Tepary beans grown by the Papago method of collecting and directing natural rainfall to their plots have more nutritional content than the same beans grown by modern techniques with pumped ground water. The last chapter of the book explains these phenomena satisfactorily, while the chapters in between dwell on the interconnectedness between native people and land—connections that are subtle, physical, intuitive, mythical and coarse, all at once.

He describes two natural oases in the desert—one where occupation by Papago people husbanding the land continues, the other returned to "nature" by the U.S. National Park Service, who terminated centuries of human habitation in 1962 in Organ Pipe Cactus National Monument. Robbed of a natural component of sympathetic human habitation, this oasis is losing biodiversity, while the oasis where Papagos cultivate around the springs with low-impact methods maintains a much higher number of species. It is more fruitful.

Nabhan enters into the Papago world as a scientist and recorder, also as a friend and participant. He tells old stories with the delight of believing them, Papago stories in which human nature and natural history overlap—saguaros born of a child whose mother was too busy playing; stories of survival and cosmic shapings; stories about the importance of gratitude and respect for the land; stories of great respect for the domestic plants that provide for the people in tough land.

I want my stories to come from places and things I know in nature, like Papago stories. I want to take some of my craziness and bury it ritually in the right place in the earth, to find a cure for my restlessness in plants and planets, roots and rituals. I want to strengthen my life choices—conceived through intuition—with stories about things that are mine from living amongst them and watching them. If I were a Papago woman, I would weave a tight basket from native fibers and gather what I have to work with:

The moon; the lacy shadows of lodgepole and limber pine cast on the snow; the shadows of willow branches, pulling the shrub out into a ball; tendrils of bare aspen twigs breathing in the night. Venus as bright as a search light; the swan stars pointing west; the Pleiades pale beside a blaring full moon. The cold air licking like a puppy at my bare hands, the sound of the wind, the "dancing girl" silhouette of certain trees—arms raised up, full skirts of branches spinning.

—*December 24, 1992*

50

We learn out of necessity and challenge, and so the hardships of the mountains are teachers, and we would be wrong, I think, to turn away from them.

An *intentional lesson from Earth*

From the lot in Nederland where I park nowadays, I look up to the evening mountains smooth with snow and to the left on the horizon a band of pink cloud. I think, Earth is exquisite, though in the foreground the scene is dominated by pavement and cars.

Then I remember the sensation of knowing the earth comes through differently when one is in nature, free and clear of pavement, cars, and human clutter. Human clutter's not all bad, but this late-twentieth century version of mined and refined metals, plastics and oil-based products is antithetical to most life processes. The sensation was more than a combination of nerve receptors feeding information to the brain—eye sees mountain, nose scents clean air and the exhalations of snow, skin feels air temperature, humidity. I believe it was a penetration of living messages, communications sent, an intentional teaching of the liveliness of the earth, by Earth.

It's hard for me to get to that place these days. I have been perplexed and frustrated, in fact depressed, by my inability to connect in that certain way. With certainty I have known the beings I found myself in the presence of, without intervening pavement or dissecting phone and electric wires. It is a way of knowing with one's feet attached to the living surface of the earth. It was once such a compelling way of knowing the shape of the land, the roundness of the moon, the spirit of the animals and plants around me, that I was willing to sacrifice an ordinary life for it. It seemed necessary to abandon material longings to achieve it. I could know the landscape and belong to it wearing Goodwill clothes and oversize men's shoes and kissing amenities like health insurance good-bye.

Now my own priorities have changed by degrees, and confusion has set in about those old longings to know, to cling to those moments when earth spoke to me without static or other interference. That confusion seems to have created a physical impediment to walking and skiing freely over the land. Not only have my priorities changed with age and time (these are two different axes, as time passes without regard to whether or not I am aging), but the landscape has changed with age and time. Our society itself is aging and changing, though insignificant in terms of geologic time.

And, where I park to go to work and to patronize Nederland's businesses, was not so long ago a meadow alive with mixed grasses and wildflowers, butterflies and birds in the summer, alive with slithering snow drifts in the winter. And, if I could stay my present age and turn back the clock to a little over 15 years, I could perhaps recapture what I once knew of the mountains in which we live.

Some of us were reminiscing about that meadow the other day (now the shopping center) and what a grace and pleasure it was to cast one's eyes over it, to let our minds run freely over the space of it. The conversation turned the corner to what we have today— businesses, services, the structures of community where many of us work and interact. "It's a trade off," one old timer said. Just let's not forget what we have traded.

We've been through winter cold spells, a time when the planet signals its hostile power, a cold dip that reveals our vulnerability. I've found it thought-provoking. We learn out of necessity and challenge, and so the hardships of the mountains are teachers, and we would be wrong, I think, to turn away from them. We have been wrong to undervalue the classroom in which we live, where the wind sometimes howls, where ice and fire are powerful voices as well as veiled threats. I have my own peace to make with my times and my environment. I share my thoughts in hopes they will provoke others in their efforts to touch the earth.

—February 6, 1997

THE SEASONS

*Liz competing in a mountaineering race at
Eldora Mountain Resort.*

A Life at Treeline:

THE SEASONS

*I love to tick off the changes in the seasons. So
if you asked me what was timely this week, I'd
explain that the snowbanks around my house
have mostly evaporated, and the time was ripe to
head up the hill, knowing I'd do some postholing
on my way to the "bowls"—subalpine meadows
within a stone's throw of timberline, where the
world seems at my feet and I can view without
interruption James Peak, Evans and even Pikes.
There's wonderful sky, a liveliness of birds, the
smell of new grass and blueberries, waves of
receding, blue-green, purple-grey foothills and
the mysterious flatness of the plains. Good place
to be—it's free, it's mine, so I was on my way.*

—June 1991

I have the feeling here that if I sit long enough, I will see everything worth having.

And I would be connected...

The view from the cabin where we used to live—the one that faced a wind so strong it cleaned the porch of every rust-brown needle—is still enough to take my breath away, stretching from the man-enhanced pond to the top of Mt. Audubon. It takes it as gently as a kiss and sends me tumbling over backwards, rejoicing in this world and my momentary comprehension of it.

But my day-to-day heart belongs on the other side of the hill, facing east, where the shattered homestead cabin is pierced by shafts of light. The old remains overlook a natural slough that has been filling in decade by decade, summer home to Red-wing Blackbirds, soars, mallards, and God knows what else lurking in the marbled rings of wetland vegetation. It's a jewel of a place, and rare. Concentric circles of willow and aspen, sedge, bullrush and cattail remind me of the inside of an agate.

I came to gather cattail fuzz to see how it would serve to stuff a pillow. I walked out on the frozen marsh to reach the remaining heads. The fuzz is soft and regular and pulls off the stalk into my hand like something alive, so that I realize I must be sparing in my harvest and leave some in case spring-nesting birds would use it.

Being here, I am overwhelmed by the meaning of mountain wetlands, and realize there should never have been a question or debate about protecting

Nederland's wetlands from development. And yet, the debate was so inevitable—the outcome could have been seen from a fast-moving train. The Army Corps of Engineers admits its definition of wetlands is crafted to permit development, and even the bulk of the old timers believe wetlands aren't good for anything but breeding mosquitoes. I wish I had fought harder, though, my feet more squarely placed, for public purchase and restoration of Nederland's streamside equivalent.

This place that I visit is a mix of wild and human history, the rocks piled up in the fields many decades ago to clear the way for truck farming. The grasses that have grown up since then, that sprout around the fallen walls of a massive root cellar, aren't native to the mountain soil. The fields nearby are filled with leafy spurge, an invasive and destructive weed that nonetheless paints the fall meadows with bright sherbet colors.

I see my children walking through the fields like phantoms, smaller than they are now. I remember walking over the same ground ten or fifteen years ago, thinking the same thoughts—wondering how to live in two worlds: one of gut appreciation for wildness, the other dutifully industrious. A blue jay is deep in mewing monologue, barely hidden from me in the branches of a ponderosa.

I have the feeling here that if I sit long enough, I will see everything worth having. I think I could open a seam and spill into the soil, happy enough to be a dried stalk of grass, a raggedy, weathered rosette of mullein, an orange blister of lichen on the rocks. And I would be connected to the thickets of aspen clinging to the unstable hillside above one portion of the slough, their trunks bowed slightly. There is luxurious growth here, growth that is luxurious even though it is slow. Something's happening where road and wheel and signboard do not go, something important—regeneration.

—March 17, 1994

*Our
"improve-
ments"
are poor
substitute
for a
skin care
program
worked out
long ago.*

Earth like a newborn's skin

Rocky Mountain spring is a mirror image of other landscapes. Above 8,500 feet, wet snowbanks swamp the land. Small brown exposures of earth, bark and stones, lichen, or the hardy leaves of kinnikinnick, are set into the snow the way small ponds and puddles show up at other times of the year.

The soil in spring has the quality of newborn skin, if it hasn't been disturbed by harsh human developments. It's survived winter frost, spring thaw, wind or burial by snow, and come out fresh and ready to sprout new life.

Natural vegetation has evolved over the ages as a protective coat for this seasonal newness. When we replace it, with pavement or blue grass, cuts and tire ruts, we obliterate the tender toughness of earth's skin. This organ has been designed for give and take, and for the greatest number of natural inhabitants possible on a sustainable basis. Our "improvements" are poor substitute for a skin care program worked out long ago.

I love caressing this natural surface. Somewhere as a child, I discovered it was home to me. I learned that natural variety, especially the amazing spectrum of small delicate wildflowers that popped up each spring among dry foothills grasses, was much more satisfying than endless variations of products in the stores. My mood can swing 180 degrees, from black to bright, if I step off a hard road onto this natural surface. I take care how I place my feet, making contact with this miraculous world. (In the heavily-used areas of the Indian Peaks, I try to stick to designated trails, however, and even then, not to spread the erosion of grass and fine soils.)

How can we teach coming generations the importance of the natural surface of the earth, I wonder. Development on the plains destroys the vision of so many tender things. It flaunts any principle of preserving earth for future generations. A whole ocean of grass and natural soil is being replaced by a sprawling organism of infrastructure and human population, powered by technologies that alter the very atmosphere of the globe.

When I look at mile after mile of housing and business developments, cased by cement, I wonder how human beings can come out of them and recognize what is beautiful and vital to their lives. Our mountain developments are, at times, no better. It seems to me we could go far by showing the world how to treat the surface of the earth as a thing of beauty, a place to take root.

Beautiful wildflowers that once lined our mountain roads have been wrenched from long stretches of the "scenic" Peak to Peak highway since its designation, because of too-aggressive plowing. Natural variety, free for the taking—a profusion of lupines, blanket flowers, brown-eyed Susans and tiny asters and peas—has given way to hedges of sweet clover (which are better than nothing, and better than knapweed, which the state highway department is also capable of spreading).

We're able to send a powerful message by tending the natural beauty around us instead of beating mountain soil to death and leaving it in muddy, lifeless heaps for all to see. This spring, consider the skin of the earth and how we could treat it better.

—April 4, 1996

...around some of those people my brain felt like mush, and the discipline of my life seemed as elusive as the morning dew.

Escape to the world of lichens

A change of scene and of pace from my more-or-less domestic routine always throws my accomplishments into sharp relief. An excursion a weekend ago with Cloud Ridge Naturalists to study lichens and mosses on the other side of the Divide around Winter Park was both a welcome vacation and a stimulating scientific adventure. It threw me into a tizzy of evaluation about time and the activities that fill it.

I spent the weekend with a bunch of serious naturalists, both professional and amateur. I've always prided myself on my knowledge and awareness of the outdoor world, but around some of those people my brain felt like mush, and the discipline of my life seemed as elusive as the morning dew. Here were people quite accustomed to plunging into the field with books and notebooks, hand lenses close to the eye. I have a more wandering and undirected, apparently less productive, approach.

Returning from the weekend I met a few people who thought looking at mosses and lichens for two days was a pretty strange expenditure of time. But I could assure them it was not. These plant forms present an exquisitely beautiful tapestry of the most emerald and earth-tone colors; and under a 10X hand lens what appears to be a few varieties of lichens and mosses (and liverworts and sphagnums) becomes a new world of related species numbering in the hundreds, begging to be put through the naming and knowing process.

Cloud Ridge is a local school of in-the-field natural history that mixes the pleasure of travel with the joy of science as nicely as a staghorn lichen weds alga and fungus. Our instructor has studied lichens and mosses in Colorado and around the world for decades. He gave me some insight on time and accomplishment.

"By the time you finish learning all the lichens and mosses there isn't enough time left to explore their life cycles—you don't have another twenty or thirty years to follow colonization, growth, reproduction, disappearance and reappearance."

Passionately devoted to his work, our instructor emitted little beeps of scorn for those of us who cannot manage to learn a name, spell it right, and sort out the differentiating characteristics of a lichen all in the same moment. But he was generous in talking about his science and a delight to hear.

On the second day out, in a ravine so richly clothed in moss and lichen and fungi, creeping wintergreen and blueberry, I found my own pace for looking, forgot the names and notebooks, until all of sudden one moss, ravishingly beautiful under my lens, became an identity I could name with some certainty.

Now I hope I'm on my way to sorting out some of the puzzle pieces of mosses and lichens. How slow will I be? How small my accomplishment as I add to my knowledge?

It's awesome to contemplate the differences in pace, dedication and attention span we have for a subject. And difficult to allow for such a wide range to exist.

By crouching down to the perspective of mosses and lichens I expanded the range of my own expectations. I learned there are lichens that only grow a few millimeters in a century, others that come in a crawl over rock and tree, draping and blanketing within an easy measure of our years.

Taking a close look at lichens and mosses was like putting another leaf in the table of the plant world and allegorically expanded my idea of a table at which we all can sit, with a great diversity of life-plans, moving at different speeds.

—September 25, 1986

The land and the life upon it is such a self-sustaining wonder that we seem a little foolish manipulating our timepiece for some supposed gain.

Extra hour turns into day of appreciation

Time seemed at a standstill last Sunday, when the clocks turned back an hour but the sun was still generous as on any summer's day. Yes, we had been given an extra hour, in a sense, of an unusually fine day. And I felt, as one might feel if told it were the last day of one's life...of warm and easy weather...of uncommitted time.

Nothing was important enough to take up that space except a little wandering off beaten pathways over pine needles and over barren windswept places to hidden outcroppings of granite, worn and weathered, splattered with lichens, knobby from age.

Aside from the rehearsed and obligatory motions of baking and nursing a slightly sick child, nothing was important enough to hold my attention, so I just sat where sun and air mingled and bathed rock and soil, wands of grass, bark and needles; where I could watch tree shadows mark off time independent of the hands of a clock, belying my notion that time stood still, resisting the march of the seasons for one last day.

Something like a leaf fluttered to a sandy circle of ground, only the motion of it was just too intended to be a leaf, and anyway all the leaves had been blown to the ground weeks ago. It landed too near me to be a bird. It was a butterfly, richly clothed in orange and yellow and brown, spreading its wings to catch the thing I was outdoors to catch as well.

In the few weeks since an early snowfall that seemed

63

to spell the end of lively summer, I have seen butterflies, insects, robins covering a hillside at 10,000 feet and chirruping as though it were mid-summer, dandelions spreading yellow ray flowers to the sun, holding hopeful heads just above the surface of the ground, a myriad late bloomers spilling into the available space of Indian summer.

I have walked over trails where the moisture of the early snow and then the alternating temperatures of night and day have aerated exposed soil, giving it such loft that small rocks and pebbles appear to be sinking in the rising dough. Overhead families of nuthatches have worked the mixed-forest ponderosa, thrashing out seeds so energetically that a barrage of tiny winged pine seeds has plunged to the ground with a silent purr, planting themselves in the ready bed.

By now, the wind has beaten grass seeds out of their husks, emptied the stiff seed cases of orchids and mariposa lilies, blown away the fluff of thistles, but left ripe harvests on the juniper shrubs for grosbeaks and others to reap. In protected sections of the map, deer and elk have resumed the easy motion of their limbs, settling back into safe possession of their pathways, ignoring property lines but not the boundaries of man's sport.

The land and the life upon it is such a self-sustaining wonder that we seem a little foolish manipulating our timepiece for some supposed gain. As I reflected on these things, last Sunday's "extra hour" turned into a day of appreciation of the land as an entity independent of man's calibrations, his scales of time and monetary value.

In these foothills and mountains we are closer to land's fecund diversity than in many parts of the country, and people have migrated here to be taught by its unspoiled bounty. But in structuring our institutions and even our daily lives, we still have much to learn to live in a way that is consistent with the principles and overriding beauty of nature's singular management.

—*October 31, 1985*

*Seems like
we can't be
free souls 'til
our water
runs free.*

Thanks for water, willows and geese

Our most basic need, water is a growing crisis throughout the world. A special issue of *National Geographic* points out that of all the water on earth—all there is, all there will ever be—only one percent is readily available to us as fresh water; 97 percent is salt water.

Our small communities sit on the rim of a major watershed; we watch the water cycling through the atmosphere, being combed from the sky, stored and released on the ground. In Nederland, planning discussions hinge on providing water for homes and businesses. Municipal water costs money to treat and comes from wild places where it nourishes other creatures in the web of life.

I believe an abundant supply of water for human beings is a matter of reverence, as much as a matter of reservoirs; of respect and gratitude, as much as of conservation techniques and calculations of rights. So I will begin Thanksgiving with thoughts of water, including the patterns we will enjoy in months to come, when snow is flung against us and shaped on the ground in a passion of weather and wilderness.

I'll give thanks for mountain water and all the shapes it comes in, including the round, shallow moraine lakes hidden in the woods like mirrors. I'll think of the glassy tinkle of water beneath large boulder fields, and the almost silent passage it makes through alpine loam. I give thanks for water, purring over widespread beds of stone and pouring into mountain lakes. Most of all, I'll give thanks for the precious and unexpected seeps, the small and unprotected wetlands that lace through our mountains, feeding a variety of creatures, microscopic and larger, including Lilliputian mosses and liverworts, and sword-blade grasses.

Water and I go way back (we all do—Diane Ackerman writes we emerged from water in the evolutionary past with our primal sense of smell established in our brains). I drank water out of a tap when I was a kid, standing by the sink with a chilly glass in hand: "Ah, glacier water! Best water in the world."

I chose to raise my kids in mining cabins, where the plumbing was rudimentary or non-existent. I hauled water in an army can from 150 feet away. To hear my kids tell about the baths in the tub by the stove, you would think I had dunked them by their heels in a horse-watering trough outdoors. They didn't notice me hauling and sawing wood to heat the water, or if they did, they thought I was having fun. I was.

I learned how little water it took to cook spaghetti, and how many times you can use water before you toss it out: take a bath, wash the socks, water the wildflowers, wash the floor, then throw it away. Every time I dipped a can or bucket into a spring, I gave thanks for water that came from the place I knew well.

Seems like we can't be free souls till our water runs free. Seems like we're damming it up every time I turn around, and yet I give thanks for all the plants that grow in the watery web of our mountain run-off, including the golden willows crushed beneath our dreams of progress.

Nederland was blessed a few weeks ago by a flight of snow geese, and I was blessed to hear them honking above the busy town. I looked up to see them circling, white bodies and black-tipped wings, the smallish geese spread out in an ever-shifting drafting pattern of open vees, voices child-like beneath the wet belly of an incoming storm.

Thinking back on this, I feel the snow geese were looking for water: the wild, extensive and intricate web of wetlands that were here 100 years ago, sheltering and nourishing. The flight of the snow geese, from the Arctic to the Gulf coast, is much older than that, and I give thanks for what is in their memory, hoping it will someday stick in ours.

—November 25, 1993

It's impossible to look at the crowns of these trees and not feel blessed by the large, limey-green cones dripping sap...

Ripening cones: late summer harvest

A new flourish of activity is taking place in our yard. We put up a hummingbird feeder some time ago and have hosted many broadtails—more females than males, and the males can be quite disruptive of their feeding. A migrating rufous male has appeared to raise hell around the feeder. He is a fire bomb, a coppery comet, chasing everyone away. But everyone has to take a rest from time to time, and a female comes to drink the sugar water, a loose feather hanging from her belly, perhaps part of her nest. Another female picks something minuscule out of the soil beds we've built from compost; the chickadees also graze there—for food or nest material, I don't know which.

A family of pine squirrels has poured into the yard, kicking and churling, acting as if they've successfully invaded. Likewise a pair of young chipmunks plays confidently, then flees, squealing, when I come out the door. We need a weasel, pine marten or small forest hawk to round out our menagerie. The air today is moist and light, billows of clouds shifting around in front of the sun, without conspiring to anything serious. Nuthatches, chickadees, juncos and Stellar's jays seem to have raised young and are trooping around with their families.

There's a lot of grazing going on in the yard that seems to follow a quiet nesting period. The bucks will be in velvet now, their racks pulsing with amber maturity. They'll be picking their way self-consciously through the woods. The woods around us are mixed, six species of pine trees growing in what seems like a plethora of pines, though this "diversity" is low compared to other ecosystems. Of the short needled pines we have spruce, fir and Doug fir; of the long needled, occasional ponderosas, and of the mid-sized needled pines, lodge pole (two needles to the bundle) and limber pine (five-needle bundles).

The limber pines are offering up a good crop of cones in our forest this year. It's impossible to look at the crowns of these trees and not feel blessed by the large, limey-green cones dripping sap, arranged by threes or fours at the end of the outreached upper arms of the trees. They remind me of dinner rolls, even if they don't have any immediate food value for my species. They show the forest is alive and, this year, munificent in this one thing.

The glossy cones—like fat cigars, if you don't like the dinner roll comparison—promise yet more lively activity. In the months to come I imagine I'll feel a constant presence at the harvest as the black-and-white-winged, sleek, grey-bodied Clark's nutcrackers make good on the promise. Already they are flying over, surveying the crop. They'll start sampling it while the cones are still green and then sit, swiping the profuse sap off their beaks against gray wood.

These birds are vigorous, raucous. As the cones turn golden and start to open to release the plump, nourishing pine seeds cradled inside the scales, the birds will be manic, harvesting, discussing the process and beating across the blue sky to storage grounds to cache the seeds. With as many as 100 seeds stored in a pouch (I'll be able to see their necks heavy as bags of grain) they are still able to cry to one another. Audrey Benedict writes that they have a clicking ritual that's really a test for a viable seed inside the wingless shell. The limber pines are similar to piñons; the rich fat nuts are both harvested and planted, as cached seeds will sprout after this winter's snow, if not eaten. But, that's getting ahead of the moment to another season, another turn of the wheel.

—July 18, 1996

The standing dead give the space a vaulted feeling, reaching spire-like into blue sky.

Shrinking inventories and opportunities

One day I walked to a hillside near home. It is a special place, with a presence like a medieval cathedral. It is a tiny patch of "old growth" forest bounded on all sides by disruptive possibilities: the highway, the power line, the gulch road lined with mountain homes that claw at their surroundings for firewood, space and access to the zany pleasures of life.

Inside that patch, the world feels different. There's no place to go. Even yesterday's well-worn deer trails have been blocked by recent blow-downs. The standing dead give the space a vaulted feeling, reaching spire-like into blue sky.

First I heard a woodpecker drumming. The small downy woodpecker was joined by his mate, and the two moved hesitatingly to the outer edges of the area. A larger woodpecker was working on a nest halfway up a dead ponderosa. What a tree! Someone's idea of firewood, no doubt, but obviously a source of homes and perches for decades to come in the natural scheme of things.

In this uncongested maze of standing dead, young living trees and old trunks latticed on the ground, the air was redolent with the vanilla fragrance from the ponderosa pines. Deer moved in the windows of vision below me, standing warily, watching me as I watched them.

I slunk away from them on one of their trails until I came upon a grouse, who moved nervously away, not quite willing to spend energy on flight. She was plump and forest grey, invisible except for her periscope-like head and neck outlines against the patterns of the hill.

For all the creatures seen in a place like this, there must be dozens more, and a thousand mysteries bubbling up and saturating the air with the aura of their presence. They are a reminder that biological diversity flourishes where nature is left alone, most management being a lopping off of what is, in narrow human terms, excessive or desirable.

It gratifies us to see as many forms of nature as possible, from single orchids to pasque flowers in profusion, from colorful butterflies to camouflaged deer. In our actions, however, we forget these things have come into being and are given us freely by land and water that have been left alone—unpolluted, unharvested, undigested by this human curse called growth. Everywhere we turn as a culture, as a species, we seem to subtract from the biological potential of the planet.

The question of diversity is not just in the survival of species but in genetic diversity within species as well. When populations are cut back too far, all surviving numbers have the same weak links in breeding potential and resistance to disease.

In the global stores, we have a horror of empty shelves. In fact, this is an image that is frequently projected of mismanagement in other countries; paucity of products, a few common items left to consumers by the receding tides of economic prosperity.

But worldwide and locally, in nature we are experiencing shrinking inventories and opportunities to see wildlife, to collect shells, view fields of wildflowers, check off rare bird sightings. The shelves are being emptied and not restocked. I always feel blessed to stumble into the special places, where the air is cool, like water in the font, and the shelves are loaded with life.

—*July 14, 1988*

The mating flights of dozens of species are the quintessential metaphor for imagination.

Butterflies: *What better way to speak of love?*

Butterflies are one of many fleeting fascinations of summer. As I begin to tune in to the basics of butterfly watching, opening a field guide to pages of photographs, I am stunned by the variety of patterns and combinations of colors belonging to these elusive airborne creatures. Moths, too, spread-winged on windows, hold me spell-bound in admiration for the fluid patterns on their wings.

Walking through the dry and seemingly barren lodgepole forest, I sometimes see a Western Tiger swallowtail flapping gracefully through the trees, converting sunbeams to yellow flight. Sometimes the butterfly passes close enough for me to catch in an intuitive instant the tiny patches of red and iridescent blue near its tail.

What is freedom if not that golden, unpredictable flight? Or, imagine a monarch gently opening and closing its wings on a lilac bush, its patterns hidden and revealed in heart-beat sequences—what better way to speak of love? The mating flights of dozens of species are the quintessential metaphor for imagination. Though many arguments may be made for their worth, butterflies are to me a reflection of our emotional and intellectual capabilities. Or, are we the reflection of their existence?

Wildlife managers often talk of the coat tail theory,

where species diversity is supposed to be carried along by the process of protecting large animals such as deer and elk. But in the case of the butterfly, the theory doesn't work. Butterflies are delicate indicators of environmental diversity, and statistics show they are losing ground. As most of us don't pay much attention to them, we are also missing out on the loss of subtle environmental richness, as modern man spreads across the landscape.

All over the world, butterfly species are becoming extinct and the miracle of their diversity being squeezed into smaller and smaller reliquaries. Robert Pyle, a world expert from Colorado, sees a 40 percent loss in species diversity in his native Aurora area in the last two or three decades.

In the mountains, destruction of meadows and wetlands poses threats to butterflies; in the cities, habitat destruction and pesticide use eradicate populations and endanger species. Southwest of Denver, construction of the Two Forks dam may result in extinction of one more butterfly species in the world, while perpetuating the relatively sterile habitat of close cropped suburban lawns.

I wonder if our conditions as human beings, our capacity for understanding the infinite, isn't cut back by the silent deaths of butterflies and other species. If, as in Wilde's "Picture of Dorian Gray," our survival isn't tied mysteriously to works of art created on the canvas of the planet.

—June 11, 1987

*A moth,
only a moth,
brings life to
my life.*

Has there ever been such a sky?

O ctober. Has there ever been a month that has gone so fast? Something about the rhythm of sun and snow, wind and rain. Something about the leaves flying south with the birds, something about the sky. Has there ever been such a sky?

The latest mountain storm was a long, slow dance between upslope storms and downslope storms: those that rise up from below and engulf the foothills in thick mists and those that come swiftly over the Continental Divide like a tide, the wind tearing at the clouds and snow on trees, whipping up a froth, a meringue, and flags of snow which travel across the pine forests like whitewater crests, subsiding again to skies the gray of a jay's soft feathers, spotted with light flakes.

Let's go back a week or two, though, to the storm that came up graciously from the east and overnight dropped six even inches over everything to the west of the Peak-to-Peak Highway. By morning, the sun was out, the sky was dauntingly blue, and I was on my way up the hill. Straight up. I'd gotten out early to look at tracks. At breakfast, I had watched a moth batting itself against the window and thought, that's what I'm here for. A moth, only a moth, brings life to my life.

I was seized by energy and went eagerly up the hill through the woods to the bowls below the tundra until I found myself on top of the world before the wind had begun to blow, a world of pristine white rolls leading to the toothy-white and granite-grey peaks. I had seen the tracks of fox and coyote, deer and deer mice, grouse and chipmunks, the wing brushes of a hawk snagging something in the snow. Eagles and hawks and ravens flew by below me.

What a sense of being there! And to the east, there was the cloud. Has there ever been such a cloud? If you really want to know the dimensions of the air pollution on the Front Range, spend a little time up high. I admit, at first, I tried to turn away from it. Don't look east. Just look west. But I wanted the whole circle to be mine, so I had to accept the brown cloud covering the plains with its metallic, chemical glint.

I realize that we're trained to be dualistic—to think we can choose between good and evil, to think we can take one and leave the other. This kind of thinking allows us modern technocrats to think that progress is progress and to believe that all our problems can be neatly packaged and left at the curb for robots to pick up and solve.

The brown cloud is a vast, almost sedimentary layer, geologic in size, pressing against the mountains and spreading across the plains. It's our wastes that can't be flushed away, only diffused by wind into the atmosphere, leaving the illusion of clean. But today, we can't put the good in one compartment ("yes, I'll sign for that package") and leave the bad on the truck ("that must be for someone else.") We've got to take responsibility for it, to admit that something is not working, to change a blue sky to brown.

We are still in the habit of thinking it is someone else's air, even as we churn up dust and exhaust behind us and crank up the power from plants on the plains.

Before I came home the wind had begun to tease a low, swift river of snow across the tundra. As I dropped off a saddle, I found fresh ptarmigan tracks filling up with the fine-grained snow and stared at them inquiringly. A few feet away, the birds themselves were nibbling at willow buds, the shrubs still half in leaf, the birds half-turned from tan to white, in perfect camouflage, living on and loving the land.

—*October 20, 1994*

Grassy Top is the sort of mountain that transports you from the world of the highway into a place of the imagination...

Grassy Top cures the blues

It's been the kind of week when I don't know if I have cabin fever or spring fever. One minute there's horizontal snow in the air, the thermometer's at 10 degrees, and the house looks like a prison; the next I can smell bare ground soaking up sun and moisture and I'm ready to bicycle or start a new project at home. One minute despair, the next, invincibility.

The war, the wind, the western sky at night: whatever the cause, I've had an exceptionally hard time putting words together this week. In fact, there are times when I am almost pathologically non-verbal.

Not only that, I have a kaleidoscopic mind. A breath of wind, a rustling in the willows and wherever my thoughts have been, the frame shifts and I see an entirely different picture. A newspaper article last week described a new syndrome: Attention Deficit Disorder. It sounds familiar, but I've gotten this far without a diagnosis, so I'll try to carry on—blaming the weather or whatever else I can latch onto as an excuse for not being clear on any single topic some days.

Sometimes a "state of the world" walk will set me straight, and I'm making time for one tomorrow. One of my favorite places to go, to reorganize myself in relation to the world, is Grassy Top mountain, off the Peak to Peak Highway a few miles south of Ward. You won't find it in an expensive coffee table book on "sacred mountains," but Grassy Top is one of mine. It's a small summit, but when I get to the top I like to place a rock on the cairn that someone's built there. Dropping on my contribution, I hear a glassy ping.

I never go there that something doesn't strike me as absolutely amazing. Climbing its flanks, sampling its meadows, grasping at limber pines bent to the ground, some of the things I've seen on Grassy Top include: deer, sticking to the top of the hill during hunting season, increasing their options for escape; coyotes moving through dry grasses, getting up from a nap when I start to sing out loud; flocks of small birds and butterflies in summer; wildflowers so intense I was afraid I'd come to the end of the world—a reproductive frenzy designed to leap a chasm of human and natural catastrophe; a bluebird in early March, claiming a home in one of the old, contorted pines; broken grass stems drifted like snow on the lee side of the mountain; a shrike sitting patiently on a bare branch in spring.

Grassy Top is the sort of mountain that transports you from the world of the highway into a place of the imagination where man once lived on this planet in a truly natural state. It's my sacred mountain—readers will have to find their own, but they exist, I'm sure, near most of us. Even the definition of sacred is an individual matter, but I trust you to know what I mean—a place to take your non-verbal self, your mixed-up self, your exultant self, your questing self, your grieving self, your grateful self; a place where you become small in the landscape but are no longer in danger of being lost; a place to view the world as it might have been, as it yet might be.

—*February 21, 1991*

Silence is
wholeness,
a living
thing, in
which our
very cells
assert them-
selves...

Silent Night:
Variations on a theme

Silent nights, to tell the truth, are as dead as the Dodo, essentially extinct in this busy modern world of ours. Nonetheless, if we can hold the memory of such a thing in our hearts and minds, perhaps someday it will return, and humankind and all the other birds and beasties with whom we share the planet will be the better for it.

A silent night is one in which the day fades with a sustained hum of dusky color. Silence makes room for the boom of owls sitting in tall trees somewhere beyond the light through a window falling on the snow. Their hoots convey a depth of chest, a companionship and eerie love of night, a feathered warmth when the air seems to desiccate the lungs with cold. Silence at night is like a note traveling to the far edge of the horizon, pulling us out there to an imagined union between that primordial stuff of dirt and rock, and an inky emptiness prickling with stars. On a silent night, a falling star is like a ping reverberating through the universe—not just "out there," but "in here," inside our souls.

A silent night is such a thing, that sleeping through it, you dream you are a round river boulder, bedded in fine soft soil. It's waking somewhere between the daylight hours to travel with the slowly rotating stars, arcing impeccably across the sky in a ritual older than the oldest bones. Walking through a dark silent night, you invariably discover it isn't silent at all, as the fabrics you are wearing brush, rub and squeak, turning your egotistical baggage into cricket wings, while your breath whistles Dixie, Handel's Messiah, or Kumbaya.

The silence of which I am thinking is a healing thing, a balm, a salve, a reconstituting liquid. It allows us to discover ourselves, to be ourselves, to hear our smallness in a larger world. Blessed are the mountain cabins far from the highway, railroad tunnels and international airports. Blessed are the homes freed from refrigerator hum. Blessed are the apartments in which all neighbors are quiet, and none play reverberating bass at night.

Blessed is the humble home in which the children sleep and only you are awake, meditating on the space between midnight and dawn. Blessed are the small rooms in which a lit candle sputtering down into the wax creates marbled paisley air patterns, causing dust motes to dance and sleepers to stir. Blessed is the wind that plays different chords in different trees, whistling through limbers, sounding like a full chorus passing through the long needled ponderosa branches, strumming lodgepole and scrolling through spruce.

Silent nights—broken by a caroling voice, a whistle of something rare passing overhead, a chorus of coyotes, the titter of raccoons—such nights are a courtesy lost in the distant past, anathema to modern upright man, who even at the height of imagined efficiency finds himself penetrated by faint electronic buzz. Yet in the mountains we can still discover a parenthesis of silence (the sliver of old moon turns to new), and then, the place we call home is irredeemably beautiful.

Silence is wholeness, a living thing, in which our very cells assert themselves, mirroring from within the fertile inventiveness of nature, the recombinant glory of it all. What a marvelous thing it would be, to give silent nights, wrapped in shimmering moonlight reflected off snow-drifts in the pines, tied with ribbons of stars. To put such a thing into another's hands, to have and to hold, to save, if necessary, until just the right moment, would be, I think, the perfect Solstice greeting.

—December 21, 1995

I get caught up by shifting patterns of tree shadows on snow, rolling drifts and shimmering patches of sunshine.

Skiing comes on like a sneeze

" I feel sarcasm coming on," says a friend, announcing a mood like someone breathing in for a sneeze. I feel a column about skiing coming on in the same way. Much as I want to brush the impulse aside, it has been building up to this release.

Over a nourishing and needed vacation, I relearned the routine of dressing warmly, gathering waxes and glasses and refreshment into a belt pack, lacing on my boots and zipping up my gaiters to step out the door for a trip. No matter how short or long, skiing is a "trip" for me.

I usually ski by myself, engrossed in the moment which is as emphatic as a hot bath. I get caught up by shifting patterns of tree shadows on snow, rolling drifts and shimmering patches of sunshine. I thrive on the rhythm, a rhythm like rowing, though I stop often to look up through the surface of the forest to the ocean of light and roundness of planet I know is there.

I like to ski alone, stopping often to gaze into nothing and everything, to listen to the wind and ponder the prose of animal tracks, climbing to ridge tops, looking out to distant views framed between tree trunks like pictures at an exhibition.

Little things about skiing entertain me, such as the waxes molded into tubes slightly larger than film cans and coded by color. Here you can travel the rainbow from cold to warm waxes and back again in a few days. It astounds me that one morning I'll look at the thermometer, taste the frost burn in the air and choose a black polar wax (-22 to 5 degrees F) or pale green (5 to 14 degrees F) to smooth on the bottoms of my skis so I can climb the trail without slipping, while next morning I'll be reaching for the blues and purples instead.

Taking my hands out of the pole straps for the downhill run is a detail I treat like religion. My old poles have baskets so big you could catch lobsters in them, and snags beside the trail may grab at them, yanking painfully at my arm if I'm not prepared to drop a pole.

But skiing with others, especially those almost young enough to be my children, shoves these relished details into the background and translates the experience to another plane. I realize that I'll be better off not trying to talk if I'm going to keep up with anyone—this is a good lesson for me. Soon I'm bringing up the rear, admitting how erratic my private pace is and falling back on an underlying confidence and consistency that compensates for the puff-and-pant of my middle age.

Rarely do people ski at just the same pace, so there's a new component of rhythm added to traveling over the snow. It is as though we were all attached by elastic bands that at first stretch too far and snap back abruptly, but become more harmonious until the ensemble has its own resonance. If the spirit is right, the group takes on the rich tones of a Stradivarius played by a doting master.

In the sparkling woods, tracked only by a handful of slat-footed humans, crisscrossed by coyotes, rabbits and weasels, littered by commas of grouse droppings and pine cone refuse from squirrels, such comparisons are not too romantic.

And on the downhill run, there are moments when swooping between trees, leap-frogging each other in taking the lead, I am swallowed by the fluid motion of the group and feel as a bird must feel in a rising flock or a fish in a silvery school, lost in the grand design of things.

—January 5, 1989

*The nights
are like a
harbor, deep
enough
for cargoes
of thought
and
meditation.*

Solstice is a time for telling stories

I have been listening to tapes of talks given by Sir Laurens van der Post, from his visit to Boulder last summer for a festival of his films and life. The man is 90 years old and has been a writer and a film maker. He has been a friend of C.G. Jung and of the Kalahari bushmen of Africa, as well as making friends around the world in his long lifetime.

I find him an appropriate commentator for this time of year, because he is a great believer in stories. The weeks that cradle the winter solstice, the shortest day of the year, seem to be a time to sink into stories and dreams, a time when one's life themes may be revealed if we allow them to be. Scrooge of Dickens' *Christmas Story* saw his life in dreams, and so may the rest of us, as the long nights command our consciousness.

Sir Laurens talked about his childhood in southern Africa and of the night sky. The sky sags with the weight of the stars, he said, joyfully recalling that the stars of the southern hemisphere are beyond compare to our pale northern skies. But we share the star Sirius, the dog star, which is bright for us this time of year. The Kalahari people call her "grandmother," and seek her wisdom.

Some of the stress of the holiday season is related to the lack of light, as daylight passes through a bottleneck and our anxieties are compressed. The nights are like a harbor, deep enough for cargoes of thought and meditation.

Sir Laurens talked about the importance of a porcupine to the Kalahari. She is a symbol of wholeness and of the eternal feminine. He described her golden, night-seeing eyes and her black and white quills, like the circle of yin and yang entwining opposites. Some of the other creatures of our land who have this wonderful stippling, or other combinations of black and white include the woodpecker, nutcracker and chickadee.

The contrast between winter and summer is as dramatic as black and white. But always, the seed of one season is in the next. Imagine, for instance, the summer's yellow lilies of Red Rock Lake; they exist as brown stubs in still water beneath the smooth, wind-polished ice.

True winter weather is a gift, and we are doubly blessed this solstice season (watch your pipes)! At the beginning of this cold spell, I watched the frost patterns on the inside of our one, big single-paned window change from scene to scene, beginning with a beautiful range of toothy mountains surmounted by coronas of clouds and a fat shooting star. Below these mountains were foothills and a frost-smooth lake, created by the freeze and thaw of moisture against the glass. As the room temperature warmed, the mountains turned into fireworks that dripped from the sky, the ice land became more rolling, then sprouted thick, frost leaves suggestive of prehistoric vegetation—like illustrations in a children's book.

At night, the outdoor wintery landscape comes to life with the deep hoot of the great horned owl or the moan of the long-eared owl—an arresting sound, like a deer gone down just before morning. Depending on the story, it is a sound of grief and pain or a bold announcement of one's self.

These creatures speak from the past, and from what Sir Laurens called "the great stone-age civilization," which to this day is jeopardized by the western lifestyle. Our culture is still vindictive against people who live in harmony with nature. When will we learn?

Sir Laurens told about a doctor who treated the bushmen. He asked them what they did when he was unable to provide a cure, when his medicines failed to work. "In the final analysis, we tell the invalid a new story." Certainly, the solstice is a good time to consider our past, present and future, and to create new stories.

—December 19, 1996

Like a cold plunge after a sauna, the winter storm seems to assault the complacent ordering of the very cells of our being...

Winter sends a dual message

Winter has begun in earnest around here. I could define it in two or three ways, but powder snow whipped into stiff, dense drifts is one of the surest signs of its sincerity. Standing behind and bolstering this proof are the steady low temperatures, the biting and chattering west wind, and the light that grows bold only in the center of the day.

I am enthralled by winter, after a weekend of compelling storm, fascinated by the dual message it sends to me of inward contentment and of precarious existence. The quiet or moaning of the storm shuts off the humdrum, far-reaching reverberations of the turning gears of human activity and presents a time for self-evaluation and self-expression. "How many things of goodness, durability, or momentary but unusual expressiveness can you create within the home—or within a ten-foot radius of the stove?" this winter influx seems to ask.

Conversely, there is the constant pressure of cold air against the walls of the house probing for any entry or against the body out of doors, and my mind is preoccupied with the mechanics of staying warm, from nutritional aspects to socks and mittens to major construction and fuel-stock-piling projects. And every so often, my thoughts fly out to those less fortunate than I in one way or another, whose struggles with the cold are more critical, and who are armed with less experience or less accumulated wealth and insulation.

Then, the storm brings memories of winters past, when the season has marched in as unequivocally, and of past surrender and battle against the cold...of my children's bitter, frozen tears dissolved as the flames of a new-lit fire lick up the sides of the stove and of successive waves of gratitude for our closeness and a little bit of wood.

It brings back memories of bizarre solutions—ironing the sheets of our beds with a cast iron frying pan heated on the potbelly before retiring to frigid bedrooms; waking up to inches of ice in the water can; joking about the ease of making pie crusts in a kitchen where the butter never softens; washing dishes wearing down ski pants with a wool scarf wrapped around my neck; going back even to the childhood winter of horse-owning and riding, when we finally resorted to stuffing oversized overboots with hay and straw to keep our feet warm in the frozen pastures east of Boulder.

There is actually an element of chemical satisfaction to all these recollections and to this most recent dousing of true winter, with a maiden ski trip across the drifts. Like a cold plunge after a sauna, the winter storm seems to assault the complacent ordering of the very cells of our being, stirring up biological byproducts that signal contentment—again, within a certain radius of the steadily-combusting stove.

But the most fantastic aspect of winter's appearance, in spite of all my rationalizations for accepting it, is that it is likely to evaporate for days and weeks at a time, leaving us relatively free and warm, many times between now and next May, when fat buds on the branches will burst forth and the last drifts silently, sulkily, sink away.

—*November 13, 1986*

*There is blue
you can't
get your
hands on,
yet it soaks
into the
mind...*

Searching out
the winter blues

Swept away with the snow is the dazzling ink blue of late summer's meadow gentians. Gone, too, are the spring iris (blue flag) and midsummer columbine, the bluebells and delphiniums sunk deep in green gulches, the sky-pilot and Jacob's-ladder and alpine forget-me-not of higher elevations. These and the summer reflection of mountain lakes are blue-coal memories carefully guarded for another season, while azure sky can encircle us any time of year.

Searching the landscape for color in winter is one of my free entertainments. I like the yellows and oranges streaking dead trees once scorched by fire—the stains may be as bright as enamel or as soft as plant-dyed wool. I soak up the paisley curls running from rust to mauve to gray, clothing the trunks of mature spruce trees. Red rose hips splash up bright as blood. Kinnickinnick wreaths spring up through melting snow at the base of aspen trunks. They are clotted with lipstick pink berries. Touches of gold seep from the feathers of the cedar wax-wings that harvest them.

Blue in winter has its own voice, I am thinking. When I get down to writing about it, I recall how untuned I was to understanding the physics of optics in my college courses. Lectures on light and spectrum brushed against me without penetration or even raising static sparks. Color is color, I wanted to say. Let there be light, and there is! I can only broach the scientific study of color with what I have been told, that color occurs both because of the absorption of certain light waves and because of their scattering.

A natural blue dye is obtained from an important economic plant, indigo. This dye saturated many of the fabrics of early America, including denim. Those materials, indigo's colors, range from deep blue-black to the softest bird's-egg blue. They also testify to our busyness with imitating the hues of nature for personal embellishment.

After all, we weren't born with the feathers of the Stellar's jays, those squawking, swooping mountain denizens. Blue-black Victorians, their breast feathers fluff up like fine-spun sky on the coldest winter days. Turning a fallen wing feather in one's fingers, one sees the shifting iridescence of this brilliant bird—an effect of light scattering, I think.

Blue sky, blue ground. Two of my children have the last name of "blue ground" spelled in German. It makes me think of deep carpets of spruce covering the land, and of the tendency of green to merge from vegetational bluntness towards something more celestial—thus the appeal of turquoise and teal. In winter look for that blue in pines and for the vein-blue berries of the low-growing juniper. Though it is named "common," it is an exceptionally beautiful shrub and a delicately laced part of the ecosystem. Pine grosbeaks (the males with parrot-red heads) glean its patinaed, sweet and turnpenated fruits.

There is blue you can't get your hands on, yet it soaks into the mind: the blue of distance and sapphire glow beneath the snow, the cerulean light spilling unexpectedly between tree trunks at the crest of the hill.

Blue in winter has its own voice. Oddly enough, one of my favorite blues is the reflection of puddles in a dirt road at the end of a day's walk home, when the sky is relaxing its bold hold and vibrates into dark night, a deep-blue ocean blue like an opening to an underground sea.

—December 4, 1997

I have been tracking spring run-off the way some people watch birds.

Water miracles in our backyards

For just a few weeks spring run-off fills every crease in the upper foothills with a quicksilver flash. Snowbanks shrink back, metamorphosed into ribbons of water which join together to jump, sing and splash down every junction between hills. They are the fingertip ends of branches that will shrivel in summer's heat—ephemeral, as mischievous as fairies.

Later the narrow beds will be dry, the rocks over which water has flown still smooth and round, covered by black and grey circles of lichen, swathed in moss or smothered by Mertensia, Cowparsnip, Senecio and Delphinium. Or they will contain a trickle gathered from below the earth, while the sheets of snow and sprouting springs that fed them are no more than mirages in the mind's eye till same time, next year.

I have been tracking spring run-off the way some people watch birds. Each transient spring has a voice of its own that swells this time of year. In one short valley, a fallen tree has spread the water so that it splits into two streams, then three. These braided tresses are also fed by adjacent springs—in one place the water comes out from under a tree root as though it were a man-made fountain.

Another drainage over I felt as though I were examining a border between life and death. Instead of starting in a single spring that seeps out from under a willow shrub full of birds, the white torrent of water comes from two separate little valleys.

From a distance you think the water must be snow; close-up, the movement and noise of the frothed snowmelt is fantastic—the air is filled by it in more ways than one. I hiked up this invisible tunnel of water vapor, seeing all the streamside flowering plants just gaining strength. The aspen and willows were almost bare, the willow wands trembling from the water's movement, the aspen trunks stretching serenely into the sun and a few green leaves unfolding, lit through, seeming alive by virtue of the water's power and not as an extension of limb and bud.

Following one branch of this stream, crossing swath after swath of gentle hillside seeps, I came to the deep spruce darkness still holding snow, where the trail of moving water disappeared. Cool air smelling of drifts and pine sap churned with the warm exhalation of meadow grasses; its grey-branchy interior was soft and still.

There are other wonders of spring run-off: hidden terraces in the woods—wide, wet, shallow seeps underlain by absorbent mosses and water plants that mingle their processes with the release of pure snow melt to create something different. Reshaping the hillside with slow power, pulling the land out in flat tongues, breeding mosquitoes and other unseen things...the whole process of run-off is like a factory, if that weren't so mechanical a word, a factory that works a million changes and exchanges on every water drop, subtleties we know nothing about unless we take the time to see and feel them.

—June 14, 1990

*Holding
still in the
mountains
is always a
revelation...*

This lively circle of spring is testimony

This time of year I am often outdoors looking for spring. Because we live far to the west, at a high altitude relative to Nederland and on a north-facing slope, spring is not so apparent as in some other mountain locations—but it isn't far away either.

Conventional notions of spring include green grass and delicate flowers. If I were to wait for these to come to my doorstep, I would have to wait until June, at least, when the Coral Root Orchids flower under the lodgepole.

But my definition of spring encompasses months of relatively wintry conditions—it includes the days in mid-February when our new orientation to the sun brings out the most brilliant colors in the landscape and sky and brings a blush of life to the aspen groves. This time of year I think feathery aspen stretching their trunks and thin branches in cream-colored bands above curved snowbanks are one of the most beautiful sights on earth.

Today I went looking for spring. All around me the spongy, settling snow was testimony to its near arrival.

On one hillside, where the layers of soil have been rearranged by frost into hummocks ready to sprout new seeds, I sat down on a grassy spot to relace my shoes. And to listen. Holding still in the mountains is always a revelation: at my feet the movements in the dry grasses were not caused by the wind, but by little insects that looked like a cross between leaf hoppers and flies.

I walked around a steep, south-facing hillside full of stubby chokecherry thickets and currant and maple shrubs. I could hear water dripping into the soil, and I saw many green rosettes busy manufacturing chlorophyll and ready to take off with flowering and seed production as soon as the earth tilted a little closer to the sun.

Walking up the fall line of a hill I found true spring. Beautiful, mature ponderosa and limber pine stood widely spaced on the steep hillside, sheltering weathered snags with their plush branches: perfect nesting sites. Robins fluttered along the hillside and darted up into the trees when I moved towards them. Then I watched a pair of unrobin-like birds dancing in the sky and realized I was seeing my first pair of bluebirds this year.

This lively circle of spring was cupped in the hillside facing the sun and protected by the shoulders of the hill. From far away it doesn't look like much, but to me it represents a natural and vulnerable testimony to the yearly resurrection of life—though how long spring will triumph over man's complicated carelessness is difficult to say.

—March 22, 1985

ENVIRONMENTAL
ETHICS

Liz at her desk at The Mountain-Ear.

A Life at Treeline:

ENVIRONMENTAL ETHICS

...the things that separate us are fewer than those that unite us. There is a basic unity to being human and depending on planet Earth to sustain us. We can shut out the trials of others, whether they are people of a different race, a different class, people with a completely different set of circumstances, or we can listen to them. We can dismiss the needs of other species, or we can see that it is the land and all its creatures that make us what we are.

Often we don't hold the political process accountable until someone proposes a highway, mine or jail next door.

Politics is the answer, as well as prayer

This week is such a turning point to summer. Looking around my yard and hillside, I see what a rich summer start we are off to. Sun and rain have bathed the place successively, pulling out fresh green leaves, and a gentle wind has polished it all to a glow just a little blurred by pine pollen. This moment, when our tilt towards the sun is greatest and our days most generous with light seems appropriate for "A Day of Global Healing," and a time of synchronized prayer, as declared by Arvol Looking Horse, of the Sioux nation.

Dr. Looking Horse sees the people of the Earth teetering between reconciliation with natural forces, and the destruction and dissolution of worthwhile human culture (and natural systems along with it). As a spiritual leader in the Native American tradition, he sends a message and invites the entire human race to participate in a spiritual ceremony to right the balance. I'm with him. That is, I believe that finding sacred places on the planet that connect to places in ourselves is essential to our present lives and the lives of future generations.

And yet, Looking Horse's appeal for simultaneous world prayer is a door-opening for me to talk about the need to integrate political process into our lives as well. I see a struggle going on inside individuals who are trying to increase their awareness of a beautiful world, one fraught with life and death struggles, and the crass mechanical tugs of daily life. They don't want to be drained by the frustrating world of politics; they are insulted at the very suggestion. Looking Horse offers a solution they can support: to find a beautiful known or personal sacred site and throw our spiritual energy into a wish for a better world. But I think we need to learn to use our political energy as well.

Often we don't hold the political process accountable until someone proposes a highway, mine or jail next door. Then, we're hamstrung by guilt over protesting a "backyard" project, even though we are better informed about our backyard than the planning department experts called to approve it. Or, we are propelled into incapacitating anger and outrage over what has stepped out from the corrupt and depressing world of politics to grab us. "What people don't understand, is that if you stand back from politics, politics will come to you," explains a friend.

Depressing, even rotten to the core, politics are something we must claim as our own. The most important tool of politics is within our grasp: the ability to communicate our own interests and issues to people in elected and appointed positions—people who have individual interests and ways of listening themselves. We have to become students of listening and making ourselves heard within the political process, if we want to defend the things we value in our lives, including personal peace and harmony with nature—the sorts of things Looking Horse is speaking to with a call for a day of prayer.

Prayer, yes, but we also have to learn to deal with the power that is entrenched in the planning process for our lands and social structures. That power has grown lop-sided because too many of us have allowed our own clout to be diminished by a world-view that rewards thieves and punishes simplicity. We can begin to strengthen and regain political power by communing with the power of nature and then: voting, running for office, reading about issues, writing letters, making phone calls, and learning to measure our effectiveness as we go along.

—June 20, 1996

> *The real
> solution
> to the
> problems
> we face is a
> sea-change
> in attitude
> toward
> our use
> of nature.*

Growth is like a piebald cow

Y ou wake up every morning and there it is, population growth with the changes it brings, staring you in the face. It's like one of those free-ranging cows (white-faced tax deductions) you come across mowing down a mountain meadow or thrashing through the undergrowth. Bulky, domesticated, dumb, it's looking at you like you're the intruder.

Growth is the proverbial elephant assessed by blind men, as well. Touched by different people, it's called different names. It's hard to get hold of it from head to toe and say, "this is what it is and what it's doing to my life."

A resident of Ridgway, Colorado, describes it like this: "Here's what it feels like to live in a small, exceptionally beautiful town…that has just been discovered. It's an invasion, physical and emotional. And it has the sickening feeling of inevitability to it, an inexorable stripping away of what was once sustaining." Writing in *High Country News,* Jim Shelton blames the loss he feels on the penchant for conveniences—wide highways, fast food stores and other transformations of the western land.

The careless habits of contemporary Americans multiply the bare facts of population growth. Many more rural counties are gaining population than are seeing a decline. Expanding human population, nationwide and worldwide, is creating pressures on other species and changing the quality of our lives.

Our concept of growth is also muddied by well-meaning apologists. Those who would rather not be riled by the changes confuse growth with Progress, though they are two different things. True, the history of the United States is one of flooding new frontiers with a sparkling tide of humanity that finds creative solutions in the freshness of the land. You've learned to associate strides in technology with growing settlements.

At some point, however, growth turns to decay. The new frontier is in saving the environment and reducing our impact on it. The new synonym for Progress is creative limits to human population and our consumption of natural resources.

Civility is another apology for growth: "You can't just close the door behind us," your neighbor says politely. Civility was never meant to leave the door open to destruction, however. Too many newcomers have raked off wealth from other places. They come and plunk down huge houses in wide-open spaces in a decidedly unneighborly way, taking no time to determine the ripple effects of their new habitations. Civility must survive in a framework that protects resources for everyone, including wildlife.

Crack an eye and look at growth—get down to the nitty-gritty of understanding it. The real solution to the problems we face is a sea-change in attitude toward our use of nature. It's going to demand more than has been demanded before, when you thought you could just move on to a new place that fit your prejudices. This place is what we've got now. You and me, we must find ways to change growth's deadening impacts on our lives.

—*September 20, 1993*

Attitudes about land change slowly

A ttitudes towards land, growth, and development are as predictable and old as the Pilgrims.

In this country, wild, undeveloped land is viewed with an eye for aggrandizement tinged with suspicion. The land of the New World always has been something foreign, according to historian James Oliver Robertson, in a book called *American Myth, American Reality*.

The first European settlers in this country were attached to the ways and products of the Old World, and while they managed to make temporary adjustments to meet the circumstance, they were always relieved when the ship came in, bearing foods and animals, tools and clothes, reassuring their connection with western civilization as they knew it.

"It was not laziness and putting on airs that brought the 'gentleman adventurers' in Jamestown to starvation; they simply could not imagine how to live off the land. American settlers and immigrants continued to import food, tools and materials in order to get what was familiar and 'right,' " wrote Robertson.

Today, economic development and population growth are still like the ships from England reaching distant shores. They are predictable answers to our economic and spiritual problems in this western locale. But in the continuation of old attitudes, land suffers as it always has, never gaining a real foothold in our understanding, certainly never gaining our trust.

Our suspicion of undeveloped land, of wild land, is masked by our terms of management and the rhetorical question, "What's it good for?" Environmentalists come up with answers about preserving diversity of genetic material, which do little to allay the suspicions that land left as it is might threaten established custom or simply be a waste to leave fallow.

Of course, in the Colorado Rockies, natural land has gained a place in our imagination, but we've done little to change our attitudes about how we build our homes, design our towns or cities, or conserve natural resources to protect it. Government has aimed recently at controlling the bad effects of growth with technological and restrictive regulations, such as oxygenated fuels and bans on woodburning; it hasn't addressed meaningfully growth control and conservation of natural resources.

We profess to love the land but invest little in its ultimate defense. I often feel as though we're hedging our bets, as the white settlers have always done. Take the land and call it yours; but bring along the old ways of dressing and driving, of conformity to a familiar societal standard, one that isn't listening to this land. Afraid to trust in its goodness, we are hedging our bets about the contentment it might deliver; in doing so we lose, irrevocably.

Thomas Merton, monk and philosopher of the 20th century, once said something like this: spiritual pulses are hitting us all the time, we're just too busy to listen. Some of these are coming from the land.

—February 4, 1988

Americans ...define our culture as the right to live amidst plenty.

Trouble with a capital P

In 1970, Apollo 13 crew members were awed by their view from space of a life system clinging to our globe. The thin crust of inhabitable earth, the single blue-green planet apparent in limitless space, showed them how precious and precarious was life. At the same time, they were forced to exercise the utmost discipline to return to earth in a tiny, under-supplied capsule. Since then, smog-brown skies and the impacts of major population concentrations have become visible from space.

In 1995, the human population growth rate was the highest ever. The curve of human population is inclining towards the vertical, shooting for the sky, within a limited space, while the largest number of potentially new breeding members is poised to add more babies to the planet. The poorest countries in the world saw the largest increase in population, many African nations and Bangladesh among them.

In past decades, various thoughts have been put forward on the population crisis. Some humanitarians, Frances Moore Lappé comes to mind, have insisted that population isn't the issue so much as the fair sharing of resources. Some experts say that prosperity determines a country's ability to implement population planning. Some point to stark statistics that show women in egalitarian societies, who are educated and economically secure, chose smaller families than those who are chattel in patriarchal systems.

Many Americans opt for a fatalistic view. While their

education tells them swelling human numbers make ecological crisis inevitable, they shrug it off as if it were happening to someone else. "Nature will take its course," they say. Nature will take its course in famines, infectious diseases, catastrophic wars and toxic exposures, in all probability—but this is not a creative examination of the problem.

Everyone is privy to some version of the truth, including those who revere the miracle of human reproduction and consider it a god-given right. Human reproduction is a powerful act of creation, but I believe it must be viewed inside the context of infinite other acts of creation in the blue-green, cloud-covered wilderness that we inhabit.

Our ability to see things is determined by culture, and I believe that the population crisis is a cultural one as much as it is environmental, economic or mathematical. Uncontrolled growth is not a "natural phenomenon," without a cultural component that allows it to happen. Indigenous cultures in a sustainable relationship to forest and field learned to control their populations; at the same time they respected individual members of their society. On the North American continent, a European-based culture arrived and went for the jugular, extracting irreplaceable resources and fueling growth. Poor countries that now have explosive reproduction rates have been subjected to colonization and resource extraction in a similar vein.

Americans sometimes seem to define our culture as the right to live amidst plenty. Our ability to take plenty for granted, to stay ahead of the swelling mass of ever-more scrawny human beings because of a fortunate conjunction in history, is not culture, however. Like New Age music, it is only one part of the symphony of culture. It's the saccharine second movement, floating suspended, without an explicit opening or vigorous conclusion. This view of culture leaves out the ability both to recognize and cope with scarcity. No view of the population crisis is complete without a fierce examination of culture in determining the future of the human race.

—January 4, 1996

Pavement holds the earth like steel bands, restricting the pulse and flow of its plant and animal life.

Perplexed by paving mania

In the midst of a lovely Indian summer I am having a very hard time understanding what the fascination with cars and pavement is that transforms the county. I go to town meetings and everyone is agog about how to spend gambling funds on new paving through town. A good number of people are excited about new passing lanes being extended in Boulder Canyon and the potential for glossy resurfacing in the upper reaches of the canyon. Mmmmmmm, smooth black tar mixed with distant-quarried gravel. Turns me off.

To me, pavement is a form of imprisonment. When I am in my car, I am cut off from a full awareness of what is so incredibly beautiful and fulfilling. Pavement holds the earth like steel bands, restricting the pulse and flow of its plant and animal life. We tend to fill lovely stream corridors with it, providing more opportunity for people to pull off, wear down more vegetation and compact more soil close to the creek. When I walk, I have so much more time and freedom to explore the land, seeing what a gift those stream corridors really are.

I realize that I am coming from a different place than many people. I have spent my life working around dependency on a car, without complete success, by any means. I've accepted the idea of limiting my car dependency, based on a greater freedom for myself and a respect for resources that come from near and far. I talked to an old friend on the phone the other day. When I said, "I'm still driving an old car," he thought it was hilariously funny. He didn't expect me to be driving a new car.

My old car is the color of dry aspen leaves and even has the rust spots of some leaves. Approximately fifteen years old, it gets the same gas mileage—almost—as the newest models that boast the highest performance per gallon of gas. Being old, it provides me the gambler's thrill of never knowing when I might have to find new ways to get around. It was more-or-less a gift (no payments, cheap insurance and rock-bottom registration fees) and it provides the satisfaction of taking care of something that has been wrenched from the guts of the earth, shaped in belching factories, and primed and painted with toxic chemicals. As long as it's in this world, it's a pleasure to take care of it and have it serve.

I drove my car twice last week. I rode my bike and hitchhiked, besides combining with friends' driving schedules to get around otherwise. Let me tell you, the more pavement and more cars we put on it, the worse the hitchhiking is around here. I suspect we are getting more and more distanced from anything that exists outside our cars, as we widen the roads and power around in gas-guzzling status symbols. It's hard—even for a friendly looking, middle-aged woman to catch a ride—and then it's pot luck on the safety features.

Over the weekend, I stayed home. Though the Rocky Mountain Book Festival in Denver would have been entertaining, I stood by my choice to consume a finite amount of fuel. I rode my bike to a beautiful overlook where I watched white seagulls in a distant air show and where black ravens somersaulted over my shoulder into the blue expanse for a close-up show. It was enough.

From where I stand, the median attitude towards car transportation in the country is one of unconscionable waste. We waste good land and pollute a beautiful landscape with the noise and exhaust of cars and constant highway maintenance. We devour the resources that our children and grandchildren may need to live. We are free to make responsible choices in how we use both the land and the oil that comes from underneath it.

—October 7, 1993

...the mountain bike has a much greater impact on land and vegetation and pristine qualities than does a human on foot.

Mountain bikers, hear my quarrel!

I've lost two battles decisively this summer. In my health-food oriented home, everyone but me is hooked on M&Ms; and my sons are avid mountain bikers who like to try new trails sketchily marked on the land. Try as I might to persuade them that some lightly traveled trails would be better left alone, they ride them for the challenge, while not so much as turning over a stone in the sacrosanct territory around my home.

There are trails that I walk almost every day that look as if they have not been traveled all summer, and I think that only the fabled trackers of western lore could tell you if I'd been there yesterday. The footprints I leave are easily erased by a day of rain or a heave of frost; I tend to replace lichen covered rocks that I accidentally turn over—out of habit, not design, though a design is there.

I am not trying to say that I am exceptionally light-footed, but that I have chosen a form of transportation that leaves little mark on what's left of wild land. My quarrel with the extensive use of mountain bikes on minimal trails comes from this perspective. I'm well aware of the perspective of friends and family who enjoy the mountain bike as an exploratory tool that lets them cover more ground, and test their skills more aggressively, than foot travel does.

Some argue that there is a range of attitudes towards wilderness in mountain bike riders, and that the careless and macho characters are to blame for any trouble mountain bikers cause in our area. I agree that a large number of the human race seems inclined to turn every useful tool into a weapon or a frivolous toy. Some mountain bike riders dress like gladiators (I'd like to throw them to the lions), and emerge from wood and meadow and wetland covered with mud, like the jeeps with oversized tires we see returning to the city, their drivers grinning stupidly, exhausted by their contest with sacrificed land.

But I am coming from a place that argues, simply: the mountain bike has a much greater impact on land and vegetation and pristine qualities than does a human on foot. The present enthusiasm for mountain bike travel ignores this fact, generally speaking, and also the fact that where one might travel lightly on his mountain bike, dozens are almost sure to follow with much greater impact, as new trails are hunted down like prairie dogs.

Another defense mountain bikers have of the sport is that we who live here must share our treasured surroundings with the many who don't have access to it on a daily basis. I am willing to do this, but only after observing that we owe nothing to those who destroy the beauty around their homes with their hasty conformity to a consuming lifestyle, who spend the greater part of their lives rushing around on pavement and think there is something new to be gained from a frantic weekend tearing up terrain.

And here I come back to a basic problem, which is my own sensitivity to the right of a clump of grass, a patch of moss or a single flower—be it an orchid or a goldenrod—to grow where it has begun to take hold. I realize my intense desire to see land recover its natural vegetation, instead of losing more to this newly popular sport, is not a highly valued tendency even among my close associates. I would happily compromise with the notions that some places are appropriate for mountain bikes, many others are not, and that mountain bikers themselves should place greater emphasis on educating fellow riders about the living skin of soil and plants on which they travel.

—July 19, 1990

Most Americans have a large blind spot, an almost willed ignorance of the plants that cover the land.

Bring native landscapes into mind

I've been admiring the great cone crop forming on limber pines, ponderosas, spruces and firs, and noticing a magnificence of pollen, even before the lodgepole pines have let go of theirs.

Most Americans have a large blind spot, an almost willed ignorance of the plants that cover the land. Brand names can be discussed at length, or sports statistics and computer games, but ask someone to name five trees that are native to the area and be prepared for silence, stumbling guesses or declaration of contempt. Actually, I try this often in cross-country ski classes, when I have a captive and generally upbeat audience. I've discovered faint interest even in that outdoor arena, where the snow has pared the landscaping down to a dozen obvious plant species.

Trying to understand this blindness to a fundamental basis for all life, trying to see through this indifference to a source of art, contentment and pleasure, I usually put it down to urban influences, TV advertising and a focus on man-made gimmicks because they sell. Giving the subject more thought, I imagine our ignorance of plant life is part of the historical trend to denigrate the land—to void its intrinsic worth, so as to take advantage of its utilitarian possibilities. That is, when European settlement of North America got underway, it was at the expense of the creatures that already lived here. The vegetation was lumped with everything else that must be despised if newcomers were to have a free rein to take what they liked and destroy what they didn't.

So we seem stuck in a very rudimentary understanding of the part native plants play in a healthy environment. Even domestic plants are relegated to minor, decorative status, tended by a few workers who are supposed to provide bright flowers and background greenery as we rush by, wrapped in our self-importance. We're willing to pay out enormous sums for patchy reminders that we live on a planet defined by its plant life. But we aren't willing to give it our full, intelligent attention.

How many mountain residents know what bitterbrush is, for instance? Early June *is* bitterbrush to me, defined by the flowering of the small, lacy shrub that covers dry, grassy, south-facing hillsides at our elevation. It alternates loosely with native grasses so that it is easy for man and beast to traverse its domain and inhale the incredible spicy fragrance of its small yellow blossoms. Its leaves are inconspicuous, it's just a ball of twigs—but those twigs have life to them and in the course of evolution may have given a shade of grey to the tawny mountain lion who hunts among them.

Bitterbrush is losing out to homes, as we build and break the surface bonds of soil and plants, proposing to replace what was there with something else that came from far away, needs watering, fertilizing and any number of attentions to help it hang on in a difficult environment.

In the U.S., thousands of plant species—many times the number of animal species endangered—are on the brink of extinction. They are miracles of creation that we've never even known. They've played a big part in the weaving of a vibrant fabric that sustains life and regenerates through seasons and natural catastrophes. Wild vegetation can be viewed as a vital organ, supplying oxygen and purifying the air, replenishing food supplies for everything else that lives and grows here. It needs space to survive, boundaries and respect. We need to learn about plants and to overcome the inculcated disrespect we have for vegetation, to truly be at home.

—June 9, 1994

Want an angel? Buy an angel. A Boulder store provides "angelic shopping."

Shoppers are reshaping the world

I understand that shopping can be a satisfying, self-defining act and that you can get in the habit of going from day to day acquiring things for money. You can feel you are leading, as a result of this, a meaningful life. Shopping requires a discerning skill, an eye for color and texture, an ear to future needs. It's a re-enactment of the hunter-gatherer's cruise through life, with its rhythms of acquisition, consumption, entertainment and rest.

So why am I leery, still wrestling with anti-materialist impulses, ready to block that urge to go out and buy? To get an answer, you have to rise imaginatively into space to look down on the gem-set planet, then zone back in on shopping malls surrounded by lifeless parking lots filled with cars. There, the natural variety of the world with its capacity for reproduction has been molded into shapes with one-time uses, packaged in the processed pulp of trees, wrapped in bright but useless petrochemicals.

Zoning in on today's earth, you come in through the clouds to view the surface of the land: tamed, spliced and diced into plantations and fields for agricultural production. You see the scars and spreading wastelands marking the sites of oil and mineral production, the deserts formed by overuse. The bright and wild ferment of the planet is slowing down, giving way to a thin film of scuz (weeds, for instance). You wonder, then, at the selective vision of late-twentieth

109

century Shoppers, who see variety inside their stores and are oblivious to the death of wild species.

The Shoppers seem not to live on the planet, but inside the malls, and on strips of land devoted to moving vehicles. They have turned the planet inside out and turned inward on their own materialistic creation, believing it is home. They've lost the thread of mutual dependence and are dancing to a single beat of acquisition, forgetting the necessity to return something to the starting yeast of nature.

Satisfaction has a component that is missing from store products and the pages of catalogues. It lies deep in a sense of rootedness to the land and the cycles of give and take, life and death, harvesting and replenishing, even feast and famine. A way to discover this is to deny your consumer training for a day or two, or even a week or month. Doing without the shopping fix can be like opening a door to a new world of capability and sensation.

The contrast between the cultural views of the Shoppers and self-sustaining people whose cultures still survive in remnants of natural settings has been explained by Daniel Quinn in his book, *Ishmael.* He characterized the two groups as "the takers" and "the leavers." Even as the last of the Earth's "leavers" are being routed by free trade agreements, we have a movement afoot to learn about returns. Not exchanges, but pure returns—living on less so others may simply live, including non-human varieties of life. Staying out of the store long enough to rethink a consumption-driven faith.

Want an angel? Buy an angel. A Boulder store provides "angelic shopping." Anything can be had for money we claim as our own. We are being weaned from our natural resourcefulness even to perceive our own angels. What we are missing is the scent of wild plum blossoms running rampant, the flash of color of a foraging bird, the slither of snake or the inimitable colors of tropical frogs. At the moment, the Shoppers take all, but in our imaginations, other worlds still thrive.

—May 2, 1996

We are
afraid of
stepping out
of the image
we see
reflected in
our popular
media.

A *nation that just says yes*

Drug awareness programs for young people emphasize the "just say no" approach. I have heard that helps to stiffen the spine in young people to resist negative peer pressure. Yet, I am sure that most teenagers—and even precocious fourth graders—must hear, "just say no," and snicker to themselves or raise their eyebrows and mutter a masterful, "Huh?!"

Bright kids, even average kids, surely see that the predominant principle in American life is just saying yes. Our lives are a constant barrage of advertising messages to say yes to useless or harmful products, from cigarettes to cheap plastic goo-gaws to resource-gobbling big new cars. And most adults do just that. TV a negative influence on your kid? Don't say no! That would go against our popular, cultural enslavement to the box. Rather, wring your hands over it and try to find better programming with more tasteful advertisements.

We haven't been able to say no to gambling games that devastate the addicted, our congressmen have not been able to say no to corporate money that dictates their votes, and our national economy is still indentured to the defense industry—hardly a life-giving influence—while decent manufacturing jobs fly away to low-bid competitors elsewhere in the world.

The latest example of the yes mentality emanates from the Clinton White House. Lift the arms ban on the sale of advanced weapons to Latin America? By all means, just say yes. The aero-space industry in this country will benefit from the money that Latin American neighbors have burning a hole their pockets, all for the purpose of updating their militaries. While the corporations will be enriched, other mere Americans may be privileged simply to be employed, with the lifting of the arms-sales ban to these traditionally impoverished and socially troubled countries.

Clinton is asking Americans to just say yes to aggravating an arms race between countries that are unable to provide land, food, shelter, health care and education to increasing numbers of citizens displaced by global agri-business. "Just say no to taking the moral initiative"—that is the message the White House is giving. It is sad that a country of our stature cannot export something more valuable to its neighbors to the south—such as schools—in place of advanced military systems—or genuine democracy instead of a commitment to military establishments which have proven themselves corrupt.

And, we all find it difficult to rein in the sort of reasoning that President Clinton is using when he wants to lift the arms ban. We are trained in the pragmatic approach and a subservience to the popular will. While our scientific establishment (and our own good sense) accumulates a mass of evidence that unbridled consumption of natural resources is killing the planet, we continue to toe the materialistic line. If it makes money—arms, fighter planes, chemicals, whatever—we place first priority on the accumulation of wealth in terms of bonds, stocks, real estate, without regard to the environmental consequences.

We are afraid of stepping out of the image we see reflected in our popular media. The grown people in this country wouldn't dream of disappointing their peers by trading a consumptive image for a simpler quality of life and an ethical approach to business.

While telling kids to "just say no" may have some positive results, these must be weighed against the net increase in gross hypocrisy that Americans learn to live with at a very young age.

—March 13, 1997

Simplification is still a goal, more desirable than ever before, but isolation is no longer an option.

What are your terms of rebellion?

After padding around Boulder for days on end (a week would be eternity) I am impressed by how we are captive to our own technology, and how the hardest thing in the world for each of us to do is to define the terms of our rebellion.

Padding around Boulder has been necessitated by the birth of a grandchild. He is my first, the son of my first son. He is a jewel of a child, second-generation Boulder Community Hospital, third-generation of a commitment to this place.

This place is defined by geography, geology and ecology—by soils, bird and plant life—by time itself. We are placed here in time, and my grandson, passing through at this moment—glorious fall-out from the meteor showers, cradled by a thin waning moon—is making me think deeply about the nature of our existence here and now. I see a lot that needs fixing. I see the difficulty of freeing my own soul from a menacing materialism, while caring for the likes of his.

Materialism and its side-kick technology have made it possible for him to come safely into this world. Modern medicine has delivered him past the very formidable gates of childbirth, hurdled him past the dangers. The same was true for my children's births by caesarean section, and is true for so many of us at different times. We've leaned on technology to keep us alive: a little heart monitor here, a little gasoline-delivered food there, a little emergency transportation or miraculous communications along the way. Modern toys and tools guarantee our lives. They don't deny our deaths, but keep death waiting longer.

I find it impossible to cast off the comforting technologies that are protection policies. By nature, we all choose life. But the consequences of some of our choices are getting out of hand. Our world is becoming hard and foul, outside the boundaries of our carefully constructed nests. My question is, how do we wrestle materialism and technology back into our own interest?

The terms of my rebellion have been to isolate myself from some aspects of modern life and to simplify my needs. Simplification is still a goal, more desirable than ever before, but isolation is no longer an option. Becoming a grandmother has reinforced a tendency to want to merge back into society, to be ordinary and available, as well as to inform and educate as much as possible, sharing my love of nature.

I still want to avoid and not glorify new technology for its own sake. Of necessity I've given up on my purist rejections of such things as: copy machines, word processors, fax machines, telephones, cars, etc. But I try to spend as much time as possible seeing the world on my own terms, tasting it through my own senses.

I say, I was padding around Boulder for several days, walking in the neighborhoods of my families' homes and the hospital where my grandson was delivered. I walk as much for my own sanity as for the environment, and I walk to digest major events. I pray with my feet. In the vicinity of old neighborhoods fast becoming urbanized, of obnoxious, busy traffic arteries, I wished we could fix things besides the pavement and reward values in our fellow man other than greed and the accumulation of goods.

—*August 19, 1993*

Media treatment of this story reflects our conceit that we are somehow separated from the effects of solar radiation on each and every flower petal of the planet.

Time to turn the corner on true conservatism

Last weekend we turned a corner round a season. It was marked for some of us by the ski area closing and for most of us by setting our clocks to a "new" time; it was flagged by record high temperatures on the plains below us, high fire danger and heat of August intensity coming early to the land.

Last weekend also began on a somber note for those who noticed and took to heart newspaper reports that protective layers of our atmosphere are being lost at an even faster rate than was thought. The original estimates of ozone loss in the stratosphere were dire enough. Last year, a NASA scientist addressed the U.S. Congress with the idea that the question wasn't whether or not we were going to feel the effects of our tampering with the atmosphere, but whether or not we could change our habits before eliminating most life on earth.

The latest Environmental Protection Agency report that earth's protective ozone layer has been disappearing at a rate of eight percent per decade, rather than two to four percent, focuses on a single phenomenon. Scientists warn that the figure may be leapfrogged in an accelerating scenario of depletion. No mention was made of the effects of carbon dioxide increase and its potential interactions with ozone loss.

Not only are ozone holes over the earth's surface growing, but the phenomenon is extending into parts of the year when growing plants are most vulnerable. The report puts damage first in terms of the number of human skin cancers that could be expected from this loss. Secondly, damage to ecosystems and crops are mentioned—potentially very harmful but difficult to quantify. The article I read failed, I think, to convey the broad potential of this scientific finding to change life on earth. In fact, ultraviolet damage in human beings is cumulative—so that our children's lives are more at stake, as ozone protection is lost, than ours have been. Media treatment of this story reflects our conceit that we are somehow separated from the effects of solar radiation on each and every flower petal of the planet.

Still, I began my weekend believing that people might care enough about their world to turn a corner, sharply and decisively, at this latest piece of trouble. Though news reports present governmental accords as a solution to the possibly deadly problem, I'd like to think everyone with a zest for living would take a personal swipe at it by thinking about how his or her habits contribute.

Problems of global pollution are often treated as if they were scientific problems beyond the average person's control. A deeper view would make each of us responsible for habits of consumption and the rate of manufacturing we demand. A more realistic view would highlight the problem of world population, and apply the greatness of the human spirit to the challenge of controlling it, without trampling the impulse to procreate and to care for our progeny.

Last weekend I sensed a time for turning in the air, something more than the shift from long johns to shorts. Maybe a time was coming when we could naturally and enthusiastically reject waste and extravagance and instead celebrate true conservatism. Such a change would be more welcome than the first Pasque flowers poking through lichen-covered ground or the sandlilies and spring beauties nestling tenderly in last year's grass. Such a change might be required, if we are to go on appreciating these small but essential pleasures.

—*April 11, 1991*

Watershed is a physical system, a finely wrought, functioning entity upon which humans have only delusionally thought they could improve.

Watershed thinking changes the world

I n the back of my mind was conservation writer Aldo Leopold's essay on "Thinking like a mountain." What if we could "think like a watershed," think of ourselves as inhabitants of a watershed, first and foremost? The ramifications of this idea quickly proved to be more than a single column could bear, but roughly, my purpose is to view the patterns beneath the grid of human settlement. Can we see through to an interlocking community of organisms based on patterns of water flow that make life on the planet possible? None can succeed alone.

Most of the maps we look at define human-created jurisdictions. The lines that score them are those of highways and surveyor's markers. In an old atlas of mine, each state with its straight-line borders is accompanied by a photograph of its export products— timbers, ores, agricultural crops. We are so busy milking the planet dry. We would do well to pay more attention to water and its branching patterns on this, the Water Planet.

We live within natural boundaries created by the ancient shaping (as well as life-giving) force of water. I am always riveted by maps which forgo human purpose and show only the natural features of the land. The western hemisphere is an incredible sight, for instance, composed of ripples and curves, coastlines, mountains and plains. The rocky backbones of mountain ranges contrast with the fingering lines of watersheds, smooth plains of drylands and ancient lakebeds. Here we are, backing up to a continental divide. Our homesteads are in the headwaters of rivers that flow to the Gulf of Mexico. In the largest sense, we are part of the Atlantic Ocean watershed.

In fine detail, we inhabit upper Left Hand Creek; Little Four Mile; North, Middle, South Boulder Creek; or tributaries of Clear Creek. Each hillside and meadow, dip and rise, is a catchment area for snow and rain that feed the seeps and creeks that in turn run on to bigger things. Over the rocky shape of the land, a covering of vegetation pulses with life's blood, like the nutrient-spreading velvet covering the growing antlers of elk and deer. From root to open sky, an infinitely complicated relationship with other creatures exists, connecting soil microbes to soaring eagles. Land is sponge, land is solar collector. Watershed is a physical system, a finely-wrought, functioning entity upon which humans have only delusionally thought they could improve. Watershed also connotes a divide between attitudes and visions.

Living in the watershed and thinking in its terms bring our attention back to the land under our feet. The watershed concept is coming into focus in some quarters. We live in the greater Platte River watershed, and what we do here affects birds, fish and other living things downstream from us. An environmental advocacy group appeals to us to be aware of watershed issues downstream as well as in our own backyards. The Bioregional movement is based on watershed thinking, emphasizing knowledge of local natural history and a responsibility to all creatures living within a watershed.

Our current governmental structures are designed to give order to human society. Too often, they become exclusively devoted to human concerns. We can't afford to leave out our interconnection with non-human lives. With watershed thinking, we can begin to create an underlying structure of responsible governance. The shape of the watershed is a universal pattern of leaves and branches, of veins and circulatory systems. Our lives depend upon it.

—September 11, 1997

Don't abandon Earth for space

Just the other day I understood for the first time why people yearn for space travel to deliver them from this planet to a new world. This understanding came while listening to a radio broadcast; the speaker was describing the diminished nature of our Earth from man's activities in this century.

I realized how his perception of an impoverished world coincided with my own. This corroboration forced an admission, that regardless how I might love the earth, it was growing poorer in life forms and life substance everyday because of mankind's improvident usage.

So for a moment I imagined being transported to a new world, one as beautiful as this when it was an un-spoiled garden. Perhaps space travel would be the only possible route to a healthy world.

Years ago a friend asked me if it was wise for me to raise my children as close to the beauty of the natural world as I was striving to do. "Are you bringing them up to love something that will not exist as they grow older?" she asked. I didn't accept her pessimism then, but I do now. Though my children love the beauty of the land in its natural state and the interactions of basic elements—earth and water, fire and air—they are at this moment more taken by the values of society. And those values and subsequent behaviors devour natural beauty and spit out polluted air, water and soil.

I am depressed by this reality and feel helpless to

change my children's relation to society and their need to fit into a social milieu from which I cannot divorce myself.

I can't claim to have absolute proof that the force of nature is diminishing on planet Earth, but I have some strong indications. Growing up in Boulder County and spending a lot of time outdoors, I have witnessed a degradation of air and water quality and plant and animal richness.

When I was a child I was taught that the equatorial rain forests were unconquerable and undiminishable. Today I know this natural wonder is being destroyed by man's activities at a phenomenal rate, perhaps as much as 50 million acres per year.

Would I be happier in ignorance, never knowing I was missing the pristine beauty of Earth that once existed and is no more? Would I be better adjusted thinking computer graphics were the sum total of the wonders of our planet, and forget great flocks of birds and beasts and unlimited variations of life forms? Could my aesthetic longings be satisfied by *National Geographic,* instead of wanting magnificent growing things and natural beauty at my feet and all around me?

It's hard to practice active love of something that dies a little every day. But what beauty there is in the natural world has to be seen with open eyes, so I think that ignorance and space travel are not the answer. As easily as I can imagine traveling to an unspoiled world, I can imagine a resurgence of nature on this planet just as life comes to the grey ash of a newly created volcanic island.

The natural world is by nature regenerative. If only we would step back one or two paces and give it a chance to recoup its former magnificence.

—*March 8, 1985*

All the species of life in the world seem to fit into an enormous, interlocking jigsaw puzzle.

The darker it gets, the faster we drive

I imagine that to some, the idea of species loss seems like a lame excuse for slowing what presently is called progress: the transformation of wild states to profitable estates, the extreme convenience of modern consumerism. Perhaps the word "species" has an anesthetizing effect. Some may react to cries of "species loss" as if an esoteric concern were being dredged up by disaffected hippies and overly educated scientific types.

It might help to unite us in caring about species loss simply to start with the word itself, which is used to talk about kinds of plants and animals and other life forms that are distinct from one another and not likely to interbreed. The word "species" has been snatched intact from the Latin roots of our language. Romans used it to mean a *kind,* a *form,* an *appearance.* From the same root we have *special* and *specific* and *specious,* which once denoted *beautiful,* without qualification.

When you see a hawk, it is one of many species. A red-tailed hawk is a single species. Two species of cottonwood trees grace Colorado streamsides and paint them golden in the fall: the plains and mountain cottonwood, also named broad- and narrow-leafed. These two species do hybridize, as do species of Colorado spruce, producing evergreen branches tinged varying intensities of blue.

To me, the world of species is an exciting one, presenting a wonderful array of patterns, of likenesses and differences that call our skills at differentiation into play. Closely observed, a meadow of yellow wildflowers becomes a medley of many kinds of yellow yellows—each of which has its own special beauty, its place in the food chain and succession of plants, its herbal chemistry, and so forth.

All of the species of life in the world seem to fit into an enormous, interlocking jigsaw puzzle. To some higher power or insightful intelligence, the loss of pieces must be infuriating. Lost pieces make the puzzle flimsy as well. The gain of new species and loss of others have been part of the puzzle over time, but a fantastic acceleration of losses is occurring—probably because of human population growth and philosophies of using nature.

In *Last Chance to See,* English writer Douglas Adams describes seeking out a few rare animals on the brink of extinction and explains his feeling for them. He describes overall species loss thus: Most of the extinctions of plants and animals since prehistoric times have occurred in the last 300 years. Of those the majority have been lost in the last 50 years...of the losses of plants and animals in the last 50 years, most have occurred in the last 10 years. "The darker it gets, the faster we're driving," he observes.

Other experts estimate that today's loss of species globally is at a rate of up to four per hour; 9,000 plants and animals are at risk in the U.S. and may slip into extinction if our habits of consumption and land use don't change.

Those are the statistics. Patti Larkin approaches the concept in song. Bordered by sorrowful guitar chords, she sings a cappella of the plight of the last great whale: "My soul has been torn from me, and I am bleeding. My heart it has been rent and I am crying. As the beauty around me fades and I am dying...what race will be next in line now for the slaughter, the elephant or the seal or your sons and daughters?"

Species loss is above all a loss of beauty, and beauty is no small matter.

—*February 3, 1994*

The news that one-fourth of life's variety on the planet is going down the tubes ought to take up the whole paper, my heart tells me.

Life forms signing off the web

Of all the mammal species on earth, one fourth are in danger of extinction, reports the World Conservation Union. One-eighth of all mammal species may disappear in a decade.

News of this report on species loss was on the front page of an inside section of a local daily, "below the fold" as they say in the trade, not quite urgent or newsworthy enough to top the page. Black holes and life on Mars, new shopping centers and unusual human interest stories are more newsworthy fare. When reports such as this on mass extinction do make the news, they are couched in statistics and even-toned conjectures about the meaning of species loss. By the use of numbers, we apply an objectivity that serves to distance us from an emotional reaction to what is actually a terrifying report on global health.

The news that one-fourth of life's variety on the planet is going down the tubes ought to take up the whole paper, my heart tells me. I know, the report referred to "mammals." Similar statistics exist for other categories of life. Perhaps the percentages are lower in some categories. In others they are higher. One-third of the world's known primate species are at risk of extinction. One third of the world's fish species and one-fourth of its amphibians may disappear. Unique plant types are similarly endangered—plants which create a basis for life in the varied soils, moisture regimes, and temperature ranges of the planet.

Somehow, we need to bridge the emotional distance we maintain between ourselves, our every day lives, and the fact that life-forms are signing off the planetary web forever, as far as anyone knows. These creatures, these marvels of diversity, are abandoning ship with nowhere else to go. Like the ozone layer above us that protects us from the destructive power of the sun, the fabric of life on the surface of the planet is rent by holes, and the holes are getting larger.

Writers who crank out daily or weekly copy should find unlimited angles in the crisis. It begs us to examine our institutions, our scientific and economic views, our communication systems and our religions. As I write this, I see that we who are concerned with such things could begin to explain why species are so important. That is, if there are plenty of birds in the form of starlings and English sparrows in the world, why should we be concerned about fox sparrows, locally at risk?

We need to explore a variety of issues and to get past the initial reaction to this crisis of loss—"Oh, overpopulation, I can't do anything about that." Overpopulation is only one part of the problem. Some people are making admirable efforts to contain it. It may be a symptom as well as a cause, an outcome of a world view that ignores the principle of staying in balance with the natural world.

We can do a great deal about the cycle of human consumption and waste that is altering the biosphere and weakening its web of interconnected lives through the creation of pollution and the destruction of habitats. We can begin to tie our everyday product use to the death or survival of life on earth as we have had the pleasure of knowing it. As both creators and consumers of wealth, we can act with primary responsibility to all species, not just ourselves.

First, we have to feel our loss. We have to relate to wildlife and wilderness not as a "warm fuzzy" that enhances our taken-for-granted man-made world, but as something alive that is being annihilated, something upon which we too depend. The sum of life on earth can be compared to many things, including a library filled with more information than any man or generation can absorb. A grateful humility in being part of its enormous scope can be a catalyst for understanding.

—October 17, 1996

We who need rows and rows of breakfast cereals in a super-market ought to appreciate the fact that nature needs an almost infinite variety...

Forest Service could save time, money by protecting web of life

I n a revival of the comedy *Father Knows Best,* the U.S. Department of Agriculture wants to eliminate the appeals process for deciding the fate of public lands. Call it, *The Forest Service Knows Best,* and put away your sensitivities about healthy ecosystems. Forget about conserving resources for your children and theirs.

Agriculture Secretary Edward Madigan says that junking the Forest Service's obligation to answer appeals will streamline economic growth. Appeals require countless man-hours and piles of paper to validate Forest Service decisions. In the past year, only five percent of appeals have changed the original plans to dispose of natural resources. By dropping the process, replacing it with a thirty-day comment period or the necessity of legal suits, the economy will get the raw materials it needs to operate faster, Madigan maintains.

You are invited to register your opinion on this small change in the rules by sending letters to the Appeals Staff. This issue definitely deserves a letter, but the heart of the matter is getting the Forest Service to protect ecosystems in the first round of its planning. The agency could look beyond the short-term economic benefits of cutting trees and drilling wells, grazing cattle or mining gold. Both the public and its managers could learn to stop using resources as a quick fix to the economy, and instead, to increase the long-term stability of nature.

Biodiversity is a sort of shorthand for this stability: the complex web of plant and animal life on earth. In this web, much of what seems superfluous is really essential to bonding life together. We who need rows and rows of breakfast cereals in a supermarket ought to appreciate the fact that nature needs an almost infinite variety of plants, birds, insects, soil micro-organisms and so forth to sustain the quality of life on earth.

The U.S. Forest Service has only begun to recognize biodiversity as a management imperative. It's still too early to determine if it isn't just giving lip service. In deed, the agency looks more attuned to selling off diversity. In a recent sale to Stone Container Corporation in southwest Colorado, the agency cooperated with industry at the expense of ecosystems. At Sandbench, the Forest Service built roads into an area that was repeatedly recommended for preservation. Defending their decisions against public outrage, the Forest Service closed the area to the public. This not only put the land off-limits to its rightful owners, it meant that people couldn't see for themselves whether or not Stone Container Corporation was damaging the forest.

In the Pacific Northwest, the Forest Service has facilitated logging on a larger scale. As a result, watersheds are degraded—fewer species live in rivers and water is of poorer quality. Species that depend on ancient, dying trees are on the brink of extinction. Loggers, egged on by the companies that employ them, decry the protection of a small owl at the cost of their jobs. They fail to see the larger truth: in a very few years the great trees that support their jobs will be gone. They are blind to the fathomless, complex web of life that created those valuable trees in the first place.

The proposal to eliminate appeals to the Forest Service plans assumes that we can trust appointed officials to think for us and to act in the best interests of nature. But the burden of proof should continue to be with the agencies, which owe the public full and honest accounting as to how our land is being used. *Father Knows Best* couldn't play as comedy today, and neither should this proposal.

—April 23, 1992

The mystery of the disappearing toad

Nobody claims to know just why the boreal toad has disappeared from Colorado's high country wetlands, where it was taken for granted as part of the ecosystem until the 1970s. University of Colorado Research Station director Bill Bowman's comment that a lot of questions in nature don't have single, direct answers, may hold true for the toad—or may not—but the fact remains that boreal toads have disappeared from 80 to 90 percent of their habitat in the state.

Remaining populations are not "recruiting" well— that's a biologist's term meaning that they are not reproducing or surviving in sufficient numbers to maintain or expand their population. The possibility that they are declining when companion amphibians, such as the striped chorus frog, are holding their own, may or may not discredit environmental reasons for their disappearance.

I've never liked easy answers, anyway. I like things a little complicated, with patterns woven into the fabric. The grabbing thing about the disappearance of toads, frogs and salamanders worldwide is first of all the amphibians themselves: complex, highly-specialized creatures with a wide range of behaviors and adaptations, some that make them especially vulnerable to acid rain and other pollutants. Secondly, the potential explanations for disappearance make me think in greater depth about my own environment and behavior.

I like a good mystery, although I wish I knew that this one would have a happy ending. It's a poorer world for a child to grow into without the many amphibians that once were abundant. Many of us remember our encounters with waters filled with leopard frogs or dragonish-looking sub-adult salamanders, our fascination with tadpoles, or just holding a dry, blinking frog in our hands. Like many researchers, we may carry a residual guilt about having handled them at all, when we learn that they are disappearing.

In *The Vanishing Frogs: An Ecological Mystery,* author Kathryn Phillips focuses more on California species and other disappearing frogs and toads around the world than on Colorado's boreal toads. However, her story builds, brick by brick, to implicate the weight of the human species upon the planet. Some of the human actions that have adversely affected amphibians include filling in some 40 to 50 percent of the wetlands in the U.S. Our recreational uses of breeding grounds have wiped out significant numbers. The intro-duction of prey species to an area can shift the balance of amphibian populations.

She tells about the taste developed for frogs legs in frontier San Francisco. This sophisticated entrée led first to overhunting of frogs in California. The appetite for frogs' legs then was filled by imports from Europe and ultimately from India and other distant countries. India recently banned frog exports when people realized the creatures were functioning quite well as mosquito predators, thank you, at no added cost to the environment. Our taste for cer-tain products can be much more far-reaching than we take the time to imagine.

Phillips tells about a study of boreal toads at Lost Lake, Oregon, where they have been re-introduced. There, researchers determined that boreal toad eggs were more susceptible to ultra-vi-olet radiation—and to increases in UV caused by ozone depletion—than were the Pacific tree frog, which has not declined in that region.

Our pollutants, the toxic by-products of cars, computers, agri-culture, waste disposal and other manufacturing, reach into apparently pristine environments—which may explain the loss of amphibians in the Monteverde Cloud Forest of Costa Rica. Some creatures are more vulnerable than others. The toad and its disap-pearing relatives are more than the proverbial "canary." They are as fascinating as any fiction, and the outcome of a world without them may not be good.

—September 4, 1996

More essays will be written about land grief, for I believe it is shared.

No *turning away from dying land*

In many ways I can be optimistic about a future in which today's children insist on protecting wildlife and other natural values and in which government plans for that protection. It's heartening to see that Nederland's elementary students are investigating wildlife needs and open space potential around the town. I also believe that people will insist on more environmental protection from regional planners as population pressures continue to increase, throughout the state, throughout the world.

But having grown up in this place, where natural surroundings were not only precious to me, but a cornerstone of my well-being, I suffer from something I've come to call land grief. I cannot shake it off. It is a darkness that has lighter moments, but never goes away. I despair of living in a world where the wild places are less than they were, where the great variety of nature, so able to amaze me and fill my thoughts completely, is becoming reduced to a few durable species.

At least one friend has suggested that my grief is tied to my aging process, but I don't believe this is true. Sensing the finite number of years ahead of me makes life much more entertaining—as all resources become more lively and sustaining when they are bracketed by limits. I am more disposed to revel than to grieve, but grieve I must.

I can't leave it behind, at the borders of the town or subdivision, or drop it on the pavement when I set off cross country. The congestion of human progress seems to spread like the spots of rust on my old car, invading where no ostensible development is going on. A favorite open space is crossed by the deep trenching for a single phone line; another cut open to "improve" a trail for mountain bikes.

There is no turning away from a denatured land, where boundaries cannot be drawn against the wasting effects of air pollution or acid rain, where migrating species such as the bluebird or warbler, heron or hawk, are forever running the gauntlet of loss of habitat, to and from their seasonal homes.

I fear that as a society, we lose sight of the great joy of the natural variety and unpredictability of the land—such as the place I visited today, where soil had been turned over by gophers in hundreds of piles, the interstices still filled with seed stalks of grass and wildflowers; where the ground was caught in a broken lace of new snow, and a single hawk on a cold day flew close enough that I could put a name to him.

My grief approaches nausea when I hear appeals to visit pristine places—"Now, before they are lost to dams and roads and pipelines and subdivisions. Last chance to see." To those who would answer such appeals, I say, stay home and work to save something for our children.

The work of Elizabeth Kubler Ross, who wrote to explore the stages of grief in the face of human dying, offers some useful comparisons as I grieve for a dying land. Kubler Ross identified the reluctance of western society to come to terms with death. She pointed at the contemporary habit of denying all truths that are unpalatable to us, beyond our facile understanding. She wrote vigorously about acceptance as an avenue to greater awareness and appreciation of the moment, of what we have today.

More essays will be written about land grief, for I believe it is shared. It is part of a ferment, a restless conversation that is always taking place, as we try to connect with a true vision of the precarious existence of wild nature. As denial is replaced by recognition, our smallest rebellions may add up to something greater than we could have imagined.

—January 20, 1994

One team of biorealists wanted to design a fabric that could be composted in the garden when it was worn out.

Reforming business and industry

S ometimes human beings seem to be at a stand-off between the instincts of our primitive minds and the machinations of our immense cerebral cortex, always coming up with new gizmos to complicate our lives. On the one hand, we relish the healing balm of land protected in its natural state. On the other, we just can't drive fast enough to get to do all the things we've learned to do electronically, scientifically. How to reconcile our love of silence and light reflecting off the natural patterns of the land, with our obsession to invent and build, or our fascination with burning energy and creating new geometrical forms?

Personally, I have a distinct bias against technological solutions. There's plenty of those to go around, thank you, I'll make it my job to appreciate the primitive, to extoll simplicity, and to explore the down-climb, if you will, towards home in a natural world.

A friend recently sent me an article that acted as sharp tug of the reins against my sometimes headstrong bias. It discusses a concept called biorealism that applies to industry. As explained by Robert Frenay in *Audubon Magazine,* biorealism offers a means of coping with today's situation as well as employing all those busy minds that wouldn't know what to do with themselves if we all returned to basket making.

Biorealism uses natural systems as a model. It insists that all resources and wastes are accounted for. No more "cradle to grave" manufacturing, just "cradle to cradle" as materials are truly recycled—not just down cycled, with a few detours before they reach the dump. Do we need biorealism? Frenay points out that the U.S. is still producing 12 billion tons of solid waste per year.

The concept of biorealism goes beyond waste management, which industry leaders admit has been a benefit of the environmental movement making them clean up their acts. Biorealistic systems track toxins in manufacturing and figure the true costs of unleashing them into the world. One team of biorealists wanted to design a fabric that could be composted in the garden when it was worn out. It analyzed 300 fabric dyes, eliminating any with toxic potential, and came up with 16 acceptable dyes to color a wool-ramie fabric that "you can toss into the backyard to feed the soil," when its use as an upholstery or clothing fabric has worn out.

Using nature for a model, scientists are also exploring ways of coloring products using optics instead of dyes. Blue fabric dyes can be some of the most toxic to produce, but researchers are studying the optical illusion of blue refracted by a blue-jay's wing, to come up with a prismatic effect that could be used to color everything from fabrics to car finishes. Nature becomes a library, Frenay explains, and must be treated with respect as a storage area for such ideas.

I value the primitive experience to infuse my life with value. Others—scientists, business people—relish the highly-evolved analytical capacities of man and go from there. Paul Hawken, a spokesperson for biorealism in his book, *The Ecology of Commerce,* says we don't have to worry so much about the survival of nature as the survival of business. It's strapped by current realities.

One biorealist compares the growth of industrialism as we know it today to a "young ecosystem" experiencing a high growth rate from unexploited resources. As a mature ecosystem, industry must learn to slow growth, conservative tactics. Biorealism offers hope, if—that is, if—we can get some balance back into the world. "Most of this stuff is common sense," says one practitioner. "It's just that we've been in departure from common sense for some time."

—May 9, 1996

The challenge today is to open up our definition of natural resources. Are they something we use, or are they us?

'Resourcism' has got to go

We live in a confusing world, where one voice tells us it is our business and birthright to exploit nature and another reports a wave of extinctions. We're on a fault line, where our belief that we are a dominant and invincible species rubs against the hidden losses of all that sustains us.

The effects of our habits are lurking somewhere beyond our close-up vision—a vision shaped by our ability to refashion the raw materials of the earth into a seemingly endless cornucopia of goods. So it is, that when we come together to craft a future, to structure today's society with an eye to the future, we have radically different ideas about what the rules should be.

Personal lifestyles as well as government policies are being shaped depending on which voices we are listening to—which side of the fault line we inhabit. Many of us feel stretched between two value systems.

In making land use decisions or personal choices, the old, dominant voices may tell us, "But we've always grown, we've always expanded. Scarcity is a thing of the past." Loud voices argue against too much regulation of consumption, or any signs of limitation. They are outraged by suggestions of new priorities in planning.

The problem is defined for me by Edward Grumbine, author of *Ghost Bears, Exploring the Biodiversity Crisis.* He calls our habit of using resources without giving anything back to nature "resourcism."

It's been the mainstream philosophy. But as a one-way flow of goods and energy, it's structurally flawed.

Even our concept of renewable resources has not recognized the complexity of water and weather cycles, the growth of climax forests or the fertility of soils. We've taken nature for granted as an endless provider; it becomes less and less able to provide.

The challenge today is to open up our definition of natural resources. Are they something we use, or are they us? If we are part of the fabric, then our compulsive consumerism may be a poor solace for the loss of natural riches. Rather than continually taking from nature, as "resourcism" has mandated, we need to think of resources as underlying where we live. We need a foundation plan that takes into account the surface of the land, a resource that holds it all together.

Some voices say we are unfriendly to try to limit population growth in our communities. We have all moved here from someplace else, so it is selfish to shut the door behind us. In the language of "resourcism," Colorado is "the third-largest growing state in the nation." In terms of an ethic that values other forms of life, the state has not grown; it has only incorporated more people.

It could be less a matter of closing the door, more a matter of opening doors to other species. We could expand the meaning of family and family values, entering a reciprocal relationship with other forms of life. On a personal level, we could adopt species and natural communities, bringing into our families those things which are especially meaningful for us and working to protect them.

The resources that seem the most abundant, including the scrub-shrub ecosystems that I love, are sometimes the most fragile. They can be easily lost to fragmentation. The passenger pigeon was once the most numerous bird on the North American continent. In one blink of time's eye, in the age of "resourcism," it was gone.

This cusp between old habits and new values makes planning an interesting process. It's not enough to say, "we've never done it that way; we've always done it this way." If we look far enough into the past and far enough into the future, we'll find many more options available that permit us to live with the land and continue our metaphysical growth as human beings.

—February 10, 1994

One of these days, we'll watch reruns of 'Nature,' narrated by George Page, to remember plants and animals that no longer exist.

Salmon is more than a slab in the store

We've moved off the land, except to plant our houses there, with driveways to our very doors so we won't be exposed unnecessarily to the exigencies of nature. We're dependent on global theft for food and comfort. We take it all quite for granted, and then lament extinction. Keeping a handful of condors or jaguars alive, we fail to notice thousands of species sinking into blackness more absolute than the La Brea tar pits. One of these days, we'll watch reruns of *Nature*, narrated by George Page, to remember plants and animals that no longer exist. We won't see ourselves becoming transparent, fading from the screen, because we haven't a clue, and don't seem to give a damn, about how populations live and die on this blue planet.

"We, white man?" you may be asking. Not everyone is so oblivious. But many Americans would agree with the Idaho Republican who said, "Why should I worry about salmon in the streams, when I can still buy it in the store?" Most Americans really don't understand how something as ubiquitous as salmon can be driven to extinction in a matter of years.

We dammed Pacific Northwest rivers, seeing only water capable of producing power, not a vital web that supported interconnected lives. We took out every salmon that tried to pass our nets, processing them in brave new canneries. We let forest soil smother the rivers, a byproduct of logging. We thought we could compensate with hatchery-bred fish, but those fish turned out to be sickly cousins of the wild thing.

"Swimming with Salmon" in last September's

Natural History spells out the plight of the salmon. A vast resource that fed centuries of native people is now a vast emptiness. Alaskan fisheries seem to be faring well, but in the lower 48, salmon have crashed in the 1990s.

Salmon once seemed an inexhaustible resource. And still, Native People gave thanks and shaped their culture to honor them. Now, writes Jessica Maxwell: "Out of an estimated 1,000 stocks of native salmon and steelhead... in California, Oregon, Idaho, and Washington, 106 are extinct and 314 more are at risk of extinction. In the mid-1800s, up to 16 million wild salmon and steelhead returned to the Columbia River system annually; today, despite a $1 billion salmon recovery program, fewer than 2.5 million return—2 million hatchery fish, 500,000 wild—and the numbers continue to plummet."

Human efforts to protect and restore populations like the salmon can be wiped out by an unexpected change. Whether it's monarch butterflies, caught in a killing freeze in their Mexican wintering grounds last month, or endangered primates, extinguished by a zoo fire last year, or the few salmon still running the gauntlet of dams and rivers silted from logging—what's left is precarious.

"We're the 10 percent society," says Jack Williams, a biologist quoted in the *Natural History* article. "We've used up 90 percent of almost everything, including the salmon. The real rub will come from not using that last 10 percent as seed." James Chatters continues: "The best thing we can do is make our first priority protecting the wild salmon stocks that are still healthy... The second thing we need to do is to rehabilitate the streams that could be recolonized... That's the long view, and that's the only way it's going to work."

Seed stock and habitat—we need to protect what's left. That is national priority that encompasses much more than salmon. We're down to 10 percent in the natural world, while we are only using 10 percent of our brains, some sources say. Perhaps if we kicked in a little more of ourselves, we could save disappearing nature and find greater happiness to boot. "Salmon are tied to the landscape," says Maxwell, and that to me is a beautiful thing. Let's not forget that we are, too.

—February 8, 1996

*Today
we live
detached.
On cement
founda-
tions.
Rolling
over
pavement
on rubber
tires.*

Shall there be strip malls in Belize?

Indian writers of North America remind us that there was no word for "wilderness" in most native languages. The land that now comprises the United States was not perceived as something separate from the people and their day-to-day lives. What appeared to European immigrants as wilderness was, for earlier inhabitants, a place of comfort and sustaining resources.

Today we live detached. On cement foundations. Rolling over pavement on rubber tires. Even our recreation is predicated on a layer of man-made snow. Our homes are built from materials that come from around the globe and powered by resources of which we have little personal knowledge. We "live here," but are in an almost constant state of separation from the land.

The old knowledge of living on the land is disappearing around the globe. The current plan to log and exploit Mayan lands in Belize is just another case in point.

I flew over Belize last year returning from a trip to Costa Rica. The view from the airplane sticks in my mind as much as anything I saw on that trip to Central America. In contrast to the scene outside my office window today—white and grey and muted—the curve of the land below me was filled with the aqua-blue of the ocean, gold-and-gem-stone rings of coral reefs and the rich green folds of unbroken jungle.

The jungle stands out in my mind, so rare a thing. I thought, naively, that because Belize had a reputation for environmental tourism and for wanting to preserve its natural resources that the thick plush of trees, many thousands of feet below me, would survive this age of growth and exploitation.

Recent publicity tells me those hopes are more tenuous than I thought. The government of Belize has sold timber rights to companies to log virgin forest and is planning to pave and expand roads through the jungle. The logging concessions total up to 500,000 acres in territory that is inhabited by the Maya people. That old preconception of empty land, of uninhabited wilderness, still colors decisions by governments around the world. The people who have lived upon the land for centuries might as well be invisible.

Belize did enact a forest management plan in 1994 that committed the country to small-scale and selective logging. However, one concessionaire, the Malaysian Atlantic Industries, has broken many of the conditions of that plan and other protections of the jungle are disregarded. The company purchased the right to log 159,018 acres for a reported sum of 60 cents per acre. It has built an enormous saw mill on Mayan land, over Mayan protests.

The Maya have enlisted help from distant quarters to defend their homeland. The Montana-based Indian Law Resource Center has helped them to map their homeland and the significant resource lands they use in their land-based way of life; the government of Luxembourg has awarded them a grant to design community-based tourism; Global Response, an environmental action network based in Boulder, is asking its members to contact Belize's prime minister to protest the plans to log the forest and open the Mayan lands to industrial agriculture.

The drive to extract resources from whole ecosystems is hard to deflect, however. As long as we conceive of the land as "wilderness," and somehow separate from the genuine needs of long-term residents living in sustainable ways, we will never come to a sustainable plateau in our own lives. Every corner of the natural world will continue to be at risk.

—January 30, 1997

Open your mind to creative housing

Witold Rybczynski is a Canadian architect with a wonderful narrative voice who has written *The Most Beautiful House in the World.* With long arching detours into the history of architecture, he describes building his own small home to fit the land. He begins by examining the assumed difference between architecture and plain ol' building.

Classical distinctions that separate the two don't hold water, he concludes. A bicycle shed can be an architectural achievement. In his own practice, he discovered that designing small, creative homes for people of limited means was a greater challenge than womping up fat-cat mansions.

The word "creative" is like the word "architectural"—we assume it means something big and stunning. We are missing out on the creative challenge of living simply and gracefully. We're failing (as a whole) to accommodate simple, graceful lives that are not tearing at the heart of the living planet.

Witold comments with amazement and exasperation on the expectations that his students have today. They think their work should stand out and scream their individuality, instead of fitting into the landscape or smoothly dovetailing with a neighborhood or older community. We are—in the field of home building as elsewhere—obsessed with self, blind to community and place.

The advertising industry is to blame for the confusion of "creativity" with a blaring statement of our own existences, as well as for the imposition of a single design, over and over and over again, that is completely divorced from its surroundings.

A home that creatively addresses maintenance requirements and energy budgets isn't going to make much of a splash. The creative individual is going to have to demonstrate considerable strength of character to search out and invest in passive solar heating, other conservative measures or careful home placement with respect to the environment.

Those of us who value the more natural, creative approach to mountain living tend to blame the newcomer, the Californian or the Easterner, for the havoc of recent Front Range development. Certainly, newcomers could be more thoughtful about what fits and about what they can afford to maintain in the years to come. But the destruction of mountain values can be blamed on locals as well.

The housing industry has responded with a looter's haste to the influx of potential buyers. How else to explain its lack of concern about impacts on limited natural resources, its indifference to the crime, pollution and congestion that accompanies growth? Creative building could have taken into account the carrying capacity of the land, patterns of transportation, impacts on services and the values of those who were already here.

And part of the blame lies with each of us who has sat back and waited for a deux ex machina (plague, maybe? an elusive bust or long, hard winter?) to save us from growth. For a long time, it was easier to stick our heads in the sand than to make a creative, grass-roots effort to protect our personal and public interests.

Creative solutions are out there, in terms of smaller, efficient, affordable and beautiful homes. Maybe we need to nurture a better climate for creativity to function on a small scale. This could be done by encouraging thoughtful flexibility in the building codes and the way planners enforce them, by rethinking the terms of bank loans and market-resale concepts.

Today's home buyers and builders seem to have turned instead to dreams of appearing on "Lives of the Rich and Famous." The problem with that is that we will soon run out of resources to build and maintain such a style. We will be mining gravel and metals, next door to mansions, to provide the resources to keep this petty and illusive dream alive.

Better to mine a new vein of design, to discover a new vein of mountain gold in the way we live and build.

—October 6, 1994

*I talk
to the trees,
I talk
to the sky.
I talk
sense and
nonsense,
and now
and then I
remember to
say thanks.*

Talking to Earth is like talking to one's children

We talk of Earth as our mother—a parent. In some ways, though, she is our child. We treat her as a child held in our willful possession. One thing I think I have learned about children—my own children, the children "owned" by others—is that the greatest kindness you can give them and the most positive reinforcement of their human goodness—is not to tell them who they are. You or I—we have no right to define them.

True, we can laugh at what they show us of themselves, but we cannot nail it down on a sign-post or chisel it into stone. We cannot declare once and for all that a child is sneaky, angelic, quiet and happy, or nervous and weak. We've got to listen, every moment that we can possibly discipline ourselves to bear, to whom that child thinks she or he is.

And Earth is like that. The ground's like that...the planet, its oceans, air, streams, dunes, deserts and rampant forests. For too long we've been simplistic. Like a knowing parent we've ordered species and ecosystems by number into categories for use. Like the Forest Service, we've pretended we could easily define the way trees grow, in order to prove that we were doing them a service by logging them. The work of bad parenting goes on, with companies like Stone Container creating bogus tropical studies institutes intent on telling us what Earth is, why we should use it up fast.

We need to listen to the Earth, as we listen to a child, holding our breath for the nuances. What valley is the wind running down? What is the bird hiding in that tall, dense-needled tree? What's happened at the edges of the highway? What feels thin?

We also need to talk to Earth. When my first son was born and my mother-in-law came to visit, she was stunned by the flow of conversation I devoted to my tiny child. It was such a pleasure to talk to him. My mother wasn't surprised—children were an instant invitation to her to soliloquize a conversation. She also indulged in her own language, which I believe blossomed from a primitive soil in her soul.

I talk to the trees, I talk to the sky. I talk sense and nonsense, and now and then I remember to say thanks. Thanks for the beauty. Thanks for the firewood. Thanks for the oxygen. Thanks for the ground cover. Thanks for the rain and snow.

I recite poetry to the world and hope it can hear me. Love songs, sad songs, gay songs, soaring chants. Hello, world. I see you.

—*February 18, 1993*

SOCIAL VALUES

A Life at Treeline:

SOCIAL VALUES

*I am always embarrassed by my work, and
never think of myself as brave. Sometimes a
compulsion to talk about a particular subject
and a weekly deadline combine to push me
over the line into daring self-expression, in
spite of myself. At other times I remember
what real danger there is in other parts of the
world in speaking one's mind. Voicing a little
personal opinion seems the least I can do! We
all need to fight "self-censorship," a habit to
which we have been trained by many different
forces. Inwardly we're always thinking, "I
can't say that!" You CAN say that, if you
believe in it and want to voice it. It just takes
a little practice.*

All of us can learn from another culture and find models for new ways of doing things.

On Indian claims to art and ceremony

Thinking about Indians holding onto "Indianness" as a prerequisite for practicing their arts or ceremonies, I thought of something I had read about the bitterness of having to sing joyful songs for one's captors. It seemed to me to parallel Native American reluctance to give their arts, crafts and spiritual practices freely to people who had just tried to annihilate them, who then turn around and say, "Be generous! Let us imitate your patterns, let us borrow from you, incorporating what we like into our dominant culture."

I was remembering Psalm 137 of the Old Testament: "By the waters of Babylon, there we sat down and wept, when we remembered Zion. On the willows there we hung up our lyres, for there our captors required of us songs, and our tormentors, mirth, saying 'sing us one of the songs of Zion.'"

Writer Valerie Taliman put the appropriation of Indian ceremonies and themes by white people in this light, while acknowledging that some whites have embraced completely, and been embraced by, Indian culture. She was asking a room full of journalists to explore environmental reporting from her perspective as a Native American. Indians, she said, were on the front line of the environmental battle. She cited the numerous mines and toxic waste dumps placed on or near reservations. Yet Indian beliefs about the land are still brushed aside when decisions are being made about resource use.

Is it any wonder that there is resistance to cultural borrowing, to blurring the lines between the source of art and ceremony for a land-based people and the use of it by people who have taken what they've wanted from the land and moved on to greener pastures?

Taliman stressed the harm of borrowing parts of Indian ceremony and using it to fit the latest fad. We do damage to her culture and to ours when we pick and choose what to use, what to reject, without the deep commitment to land and land-based values. The sacredness of life, the way, is all-inclusive in her view; we dilute it at our risk.

I think we need to be cautious in assessing Indian claims to authenticity. Some of us may feel, rightly so, that we have earned a right to be part of Indian culture. All of us can learn from another culture and find models for new ways of doing things. Many artists and craftspeople produce authentic works of art in their own right, in ways that parallel Indian arts and crafts. But we need to respect the depth of another culture and not debase it through careless imitation or appropriation.

In the interest of not just borrowing part, let me go back to the psalm. It ends in a bitter curse on the captors of the people of Zion, a fanatic remembrance of the land and a promise not to forgive those who had taken them away from it. Contemporary American society, where we are all placed in time, has lost track of the depth of feeling that is in the psalm. My belief is that traditional Indians are trying to preserve the depth of their experience, to protect it from erosion by our easy-going give-and-take, pick-and-choose values. Let us respect that and negotiate from there.

—*May 26, 1994*

It is medicine from plants; and it is, in my best (recreational) experiences with it, a caring medicine about plants.

Bring on the (medicinal) pot

I am sometimes slow to make connections, and it has taken me awhile to consider that the battle being waged to make marijuana available for medicinal purposes could relate to me. Marijuana reportedly eases the chronic pain of arthritis, and what a blessing that must be. And, one only has to know one older woman who is willing to go to the streets to buy marijuana to deal with her chemotherapy treatments, though pot has never been part of her life before, to know that marijuana has a real and perceived benefit to Americans.

Very good arguments can be made for the legal use of marijuana as medicine, as well as for the legal cultivation of hemp for agricultural purposes, providing fiber for clothes, rope, paper and biomass for energy. Opponents of legalization usually trivialize the practical uses of the plant and attempt to prove they are a screen to legalize the recreational use of the drug. It is difficult, too, for advocates of legalization to stick to practical uses, because the drug laws so perversely discriminate against marijuana. Easily cultivated by individuals, its most heinous crime seems to be its potential to circumvent big brother's control.

The debate has been raised again, with voters in California and Arizona approving the use of marijuana if prescribed by a medical doctor. Voters passed the initiatives by large margins. The federal government in turn has threatened to prosecute doctors for prescribing something other than the sanctioned products of large drug companies. This strikes some as a federal intrusion into states' rights.

The persecution of doctors and patients is being led by people like Orrin Hatch. Senator Hatch of Utah may have had some good ideas in his lifetime, but from where I view him, he seems dedicated to imposing his patriarchal, puritanical and prohibitive politics on the rest of us, in the name of a moral righteousness which is coldly indifferent to individual souls.

Pot, colloquially speaking, is a pharmaceutical in the traditional sense of the word. It is medicine from plants; and it is, in my best (recreational) experiences with it, a caring medicine about plants. Smoking pot always sent me outdoors to appreciate the sensational botanical world we live in. That, too, seems like a heretical function, for if we actually cared about the plant life of the planet, we'd be shaking our fists in outrage a lot more often.

Federal law seems dedicated to making a self-sufficient act, like growing one's own drug to treat oneself, a crime. In contrast, the systematic encouragement of a populace chronically dependent on the pharmaceuticals industry is virtually subsidized by government. Yes, there are times when a pill does the job. If the same is true of marijuana—smoked in a joint, sipped in a tea or ingested in chocolate chip cookies—I say "go for it."

Maybe a hit of pot would ease my pain, but I'm not tempted to try, having reached a friendly separation with the drug many years ago. It's not its illegality that makes it unavailable to me, though that puts a smear on a perfectly good plant. It's that I, as a sovereign individual, make that choice. We have so many societally-sanctioned death traps, like gambling, tobacco and alcohol, it seems strange to me that the feds go to so much trouble over this potential pothole in the road.

The feds have backed off one degree, promising an unbiased study of the medicinal properties of marijuana. Let's hope this is a step in the direction of a sane policy towards a plant that has been unnecessarily demonized. I would like a sense of personal freedom to survive, freedom to vote my conscience for a compassionate use of a genuine resource. Yep, the fuss about pot relates to me.

—January 16, 1997

Another approach to alcoholism, one that co-exists with genetic and brain chemistry explana-tions, labels alcoholism as a family disease.

Suppose we listed the cause of death?

Shortly after the celebrated Liberace died, possibly of AIDS, I heard a discussion between newsmen on obituaries and manners. While one editor tended to respect privacy and family sensitivities, another editor suggested news media might be withholding pertinent information by not listing cause of death in most cases. The public was entitled to know how many people were dying of AIDS or cancer, he argued, these diseases being linked to the public health in general.

I wonder if the same arguments would ensue in the case of death by alcoholism. I have had the uncomfortable experience more than once of seeing friends and acquaintances visibly suffering from alcoholism slip from sight only to reappear in print under obituary headings in the newspaper. Suicide, cancer, motor vehicle accidents thinly veil the real culprit in many deaths. Head injuries, for example, are complicated and exacerbated by alcoholism.

It strikes me that alcoholism is one of the most taboo subjects that exists in our society. Cancer was once a hush-hush illness, until people like Elizabeth Kubler Ross and many individual sufferers humanely lifted the curtain that had been pulled across the wasting disease.

We need a similar, humane exposure of the nature and consequences of alcoholism. It is still too closely associated with moral judgments and family tensions to be freely discussed as a disease. Like other illnesses, it is progressive—that is, it gets worse and doesn't just go away—and unless checked, ends in death.

Part of our schizophrenic attitude towards alcoholism stems from the fact that drinking alcoholic beverages in moderation can be harmless or possibly beneficial to some and addictive and eventually lethal to others. A Denver expert, Jack Mumey, explains there is a clearly established genetic link for transmitting the disease, one that is pinpointed by the presence of THIQ—tetrahydroisoquinoline—in the brain. THIQ creates a physiological demand for alcohol. Alcoholic predilection also can be created in the fetus in the womb by a drinking mother.

Another approach to alcoholism, one that coexists with genetic and brain chemistry explanations, labels alcoholism as a family disease. It affects all members of a family with an alcoholic in it, and non-alcoholic family members can inadvertently contribute to the alcoholism of another family member by a variety of behaviors. Numerous studies support theories of both the physical transmission of the disease and psychological factors leading to the development of alcoholism. One expert identifies depression, dependency and denial as warning signs.

Listing alcoholism as cause of death in obituary columns would be an impossibly harsh way to overcome the denial syndrome we seem to suffer as a society. But as in the case of AIDS deaths, we are entitled to know about this unrelenting killer. With the recognition of its prevalence might also come a new optimism about curing the disease and creating harmony inside and beyond the family.

—*June 18, 1987*

Families don't exist in a vacuum, and communities have strengths besides their schools.

Socialization has holes in it

The idea of home schooling seems to elicit strong responses from many Americans. Full of self-congratulations for our "individuality," we react fearfully to the idea that children might grow up without the benefit of that great American homogenizer, the classroom.

Much can be said in favor of institutional schooling. Much can be said in favor of the American experience in general. But there are times when the argument for either is so heavily weighted to one side that I choose to question American infallibility and to come to the defense of parents who are educating their children outside the traditional classroom.

Could it be that the majority of us, molded by the enormous weight of crass societal opinion from kindergarten until we didn't even notice it any more, react jealously to the idea that some children might be spared the pressure to conform that's touted as "socialization?"

We might ask if institutions have a monopoly on providing socialization, and where this process has gotten us. Americans are a nice bunch of people. But we are naively disposed towards the harsh realities of politics and environment. Advertisers and policy makers play daily on the predictable responses of a well socialized population, using carefully chosen words and images that appeal to the team player in each of us, to that part of us that decided, long ago, to get along rather than call our own shots.

Socialization could be at the root of some serious problems. I think, for instance, of the failure of the public in general to question threats to constitutional democracy in the U.S. A well socialized public was content to watch the Iran-Contra affair and Ollie North's antics—including allegations of a plan to suspend the Bill of Rights—as if it were a school scandal involving popular class members. Americans view military actions as if they were football games and are simply too polite to voice suspicion about our government's role in El Salvador or the CIA connection to drug smuggling.

Our progress in alternative energy technology has been hampered by the necessity to look and act like everyone else while we try to make wind or solar power take the place of enormous generating facilities. We heat our schools to cater to fashion, not necessarily to cold-country dress. The predominantly negative response to home schooling is a good indication of the kind of pressure that we exert on alternatives as a whole; it calls to mind Ralph Waldo Emerson's verdict on society: "It loves not realities and creators, but names and customs."

Families don't exist in a vacuum and communities have strengths besides their schools. Life goes on outside the compartmentalized structure of school buildings. Or do we simply feel a humane need to condition our young to living indoors to someone else's agenda for the better part of their lives?

After I'd begun this column, I read David Guterson's defense of home schooling in the November 1990 *Harper's* magazine. A school teacher who keeps his own children at home during the day, he skillfully reinforced what I had to say. He points out that as a group home-schooled children score above average on standardized academic tests, and psychological testing proves them well adjusted. He describes his children's social lives as "vigorous and sane."

I'm not claiming that home schooling is the solution to all our problems, but that until we open our minds to radical alternatives, socialization isn't worth the paper it is printed on: tomorrow's citizens.

—*December 20, 1990*

154

No healing, no weaving back together of lives or society takes place when the switch is thrown.

When the killing has to stop

I am sitting by Boulder Creek, in an absence of fear. How good it feels to be free of the fear of sudden, senseless death. The sound of running water, the gentle reflection of leaves and a green energy to the air easily fills the void.

Last Friday night was a different matter. A killer was on the loose—a man who had probably traveled in the mountains near my home, a person who apparently had no built-in restraint to pointing a weapon at a stranger and pulling the trigger.

The terror of his spree affected many people, some in truly terrible ways, even after the suspect in four shooting deaths had been apprehended. I thought of the compassionate and service-minded sheriff's officers who might be on duty, looking for a man who was trigger-happy and armed with lethal force. I imagined what their families must be feeling, and felt for those who had died, lost friends or family member, or been injured in the violence.

With great relief I heard a suspect had been caught. Now the killing could stop. But in the aftermath of the tragedy, talk of the death penalty has been heard, assuming the suspect is found guilty of murder.

The discussion raises the specter of another killing, a judicial execution, a legal murder in which we all share a small, considered burden for the deed. As long as the death penalty is legal in the United States, individual criminals will open the debate about the appropriateness of this punishment. "Surely, in this case...," voices will cry out to justify the taking of one more life.

To my mind, it would be better if there were no death penalty and the punishment of life imprisonment were the final recourse in the most heinous crimes. As long as the death penalty is on the books, grave injustices will be done in the name of this ultimate, stern punishment.

The United Nations General Assembly resolved last December to work for an international ban on the death penalty. A majority of voices thought that would be an appropriate step towards the enhancement of human dignity worldwide. The U.S. is the only western country—and in the company of the U.S.S.R., China, South Africa and Iran—that sanctions death as punishment.

Since 1977 there have been 128 executions in the U.S. A one-line statistic in *Harper's* magazine reads: "The number of Americans sentenced to death since 1900 who were later found innocent: 139." That suggests a potential for a large margin of error. Studies show repeatedly that the "justice" of the death penalty is overwhelmingly applied to the poor and minorities, to the most vulnerable and not necessarily to those whose crimes are most offensive to human sensibility.

Other studies show the death penalty does not deter violent crime; rather, there is a correlation between publicized executions and an increase in violent crime. The death penalty—which Americans increasingly support these days—takes the lives of those who may be innocent, those who may be truly rehabilitated or tragically impaired, and doesn't always do it neatly. When execution equipment malfunctions, those we have chosen to kill as painlessly as possible suffer for extended periods of time. When this happens, we close ranks with torturers.

No healing, no weaving back together of lives or society takes place when the switch is thrown. As long as the death penalty stands as legal punishment in the U.S., fear and violence continue to be part of the fabric, no matter how much we'd hoped for some relief.

—August 30, 1990

...we can discover that a single, focused issue preserves a range of values for all of us.

Sacred geography touches all

When I first read about Arkansas Mountain, I wanted to steer clear of the issue. I sensed the acrimonious potential in the claim by some that it was a sacred site for Native Americans, the rebuff by others that "nah, it wasn't anything special." But something pulled me in. The way my mother would start to untie one knot in a tangled ball of string and end up sitting for hours making order, knowing that some general satisfaction would accrue, I started calling people and reading the literature that came my way.

I have been touched by the claims that many sites—unheralded, unmarked by bones or arrowheads—are sacred in our mountains and deserving of protection for the practice of Native American religion. As skeptics, we can view sacred site status as a technicality to obstruct "legitimate" development. Or we can discover that a single, focused issue preserves a range of values for all of us.

The importance of sacred geography in the Front Range is just gaining attention, writes archaeologist Jim Benedict. He has studied a well-documented prehistoric location, Old Man Mountain, near Estes Park. "The view from its summit is spectacular," he writes, "and the diversity of plant communities on its slick rock slopes turns a spiral ascent of the mountain into a metaphor for the annual rounds of early people." Benedict found no archaeological evidence at the summit, but found artifacts along the way, including cobbles and boulders that he hypothesized were carried up from the valleys by Indians to show dedication to their quests.

Anthropologist Deward Walker explains that sacred sites exist for mobile hunting societies; they've kept individual locations alive in myth, story and ceremony as places to access spiritual understanding and places to pay respect.

Walker writes that in Native American religion, the sacred exists in all phenomenon. "Accessing this sacred attribute is a major ritual goal found in all American Indian cultures and entails actually entering sacredness rather than merely praying to it or propitiating it." Dreams or visions reveal "access points or portals." Sacred sites often have distinguishing views or physical features, and are visited at certain times more frequently than others: dawn, dusk, equinox and solstice.

This year Congress is considering a bill to strengthen Native American religious rights, including protecting sacred sites. Historian Patricia Limerick writes in this summer's Native American Rights Fund newsletter:

"The challenge to Indian religions today can come in the form of a long, detailed report from a federal land management agency, advocating development of a particular site and treating an Indian religious ceremony, centered on that site as a quaint, colorful but dismissable relic of a lost time. Undramatic and indirect as this bureaucratic behavior may seem, its effect on religious practices may be nearly as destructive as the direct attacks of the late 19th century.

"Some of the injuries of the past are irreversible, beyond repair or redemption. But on this question there are meaningful choices still to be made," writes Limerick. "Let the Indians know, the new message would read, that the power of Government now stands behind them, and behind their right to religious freedom."

We protect something for all of us when we protect Native American religious rights. Indian practices are often individual quests. They epitomize a spiritual freedom that does not conform to majority standards; they rely on a connection to the environment that was intentionally severed by our white predecessors. They are part of an ancient living on this land.

—September 9, 1993

Indecisive about the future, anxious about broad issues of unequal living standards around the world and deteriorating environment, many Americans prefer not to know too much.

Let's not silence ourselves

I have been thinking about how much easier it would be to deal with censorship if it were just a matter of inky black blocks intruding on the pages of newspaper, or bleeps over the air—obvious cases of words deleted from our hearing or vision, or pictures scrambled by an evil outside force. Censorship is more like a progressive disease, a slow invasion into the vital organs of society that is heading for the power center of our minds. Censorship doesn't erase us immediately, it simply leaves us vacant and bland, disabled as citizens, the curtain drawn as much by our own hand as by agents outside of us.

Media coverage of the Gulf War falls into the category of "the censorship of indecision," in Kay Boyle's words, as much as to an active principle of silencing writers and other reporters. After the war, General Colin Powell chided the press for its failure. Its job, he declared, was to be adversarial—that's how a democracy insures civilian control. At its outset, Walter Cronkite pleaded quietly: "Americans who take an anti-war stance do so out of an equally strong love of their country and they are troubled by what they see as a serious mistake in policy."

The press, confronted by a complex story—including past U.S. support for Saddam Hussein, the complexities of Islam and oil, an active protest movement at home and abroad, Pentagon control of the news—gave in to easy-way-out journalism. Why else, as

Newsday writer Thomas Collins wondered, does "an ostensibly aggressive press suddenly roll over and play dead?"

Some people I've heard from liked it that way. Indecisive about the future, anxious about broad issues of unequal living standards around the world and deteriorating environment, many Americans prefer not to know too much. This could also be called the censorship of blissful ignorance.

In other forms of censorship, public funding nooses lie in wait for challenges to contemporary prejudices. Channel 12 TV—an excellent local station—feels that threat as do all who receive funds from the federal government. Self-appointed censors are bullying Congress to withhold funds from forums that make 'offensive' material available. Unfortunately, the definition of offensive is not open for public discussion. Pledge support for this station and other public stations helps to keep the discussion alive.

Eroding access to government records via The Freedom of Information Act has been an ongoing censorship by the Reagan and Bush administrations, so that many attempts to view actions by government officials actually do come with names, sentences and paragraphs blacked out.

But the most insidious censorship is self-censorship. We begin to believe that if we can't say anything nice, we shouldn't say anything at all, or we fear seeming different from an ever narrowing norm of behavior and opinions. We fail to see that racism and sexism aren't just pointing fingers at someone else; each of us is vulnerable to the fear that we will be somehow unacceptable to the name-calling majority.

Some people never seem to see that the censor risks becoming the censored and that silence, or complacent agreement, is a winding sheet suffocating the potential of every man. The truth has always been hard to take, hard to speak; the easy way out is not, I hope, an American tradition.

—August 1, 1991

Irritating words create a pearl of truth

A recent letter writer has suggested that responsibility and freedom of the press are tightly bonded. "Free press without responsibility is insanity," he wrote. I'd like to question that thesis, while mentioning in passing that I think there is a strong personal commitment to responsibility at *The Mountain-Ear.*

I try to write responsibly, but I'm not sure that is always the right course. Sometimes I think it's better to let fly, and I give many columnists credit for their flair and bravery in this department. I think the unpredictable and words that are not always classifiable as "responsible" are at the heart of a free press.

When our founding fathers came up with the idea of a free press they didn't get there from the assumption that everything that got into print would be received by gullible peasants as God's truth. They got there from the assumption that the men and women of this country had good heads on their shoulders and could sort it out for themselves.

I think a free press should carry words to people's minds for them to sift for truth. The more words you sift, the more likely you are to come up with something valuable and original. It may be an awful lot of dross has to pass over the screen, but if that is what it takes, so be it.

In the history of mining in Colorado men have moved mountains—hefted, shoveled, sifted and milled tons upon tons of apparently worthless rock—for the sake of a few grains of gold. Don't we have the patience, I wonder, to make the same search for truth? Or consider another analogy, that words come along in a stream and somewhere along the line a pearl of truth is created out of an irritating, unfathomable linguistic connection.

—March 10, 1988

We take 'The News' as served

In a cynical moment a sentence came to me and clamped on like a nasty terrier: "News is the opium of the people, and commentary the chaser." I guess I had overdosed on Channels 4 and 7, *The Daily Camera,* and the comforting drone of the radio voices crying the latest in murders, military gains and defeats, economic disasters, etc., etc.

It occurred to me that we are inundated by this form of communication we call "The News," and that we sweeten the drowning only superficially by talking, writing and reading about it as though it were something real. While in fact it is a diversion, laced with mini-dramas called "ads," drawing our attention away from the real substance of our lives and of our planet, scrambling the sounds of the real world that beg to come into our homes and be heard.

As usual, I had to back off this extreme view, unclamp my jaw of the angry idea attached to my thinking, to try to analyze the problem. It's a three-part concern that 1) "The News" is marketed to us rather than simply told, 2) as listeners and learners we show an interest in events only when they reach crisis proportions, and 3) some of the time we spend on "The News" should probably go to a better understanding of our natural environment, which is the root of our existence and subsequently some of our problems.

We are so passive about the news. We take it as it is served, and if we don't like it, we get indignant and practice inflamed speech. But rarely do we go to the library to learn more, call our Congressman, discuss issues openly and in depth, make a commitment to dig more deeply into some aspect that touches us most.

Most of our news comes to us as entertainment. Are we defused by the overlapping entertainment values of "Star Wars" and "Cola Wars?" The so-called Cola Wars were really an expensive hype where the basic change of ingredients in "New Coke" were cheaper corn-sweeteners replacing sugar and less real vanilla. We could have saved a lot of air time if that had been admitted first. "Star Wars" is an expensive technological fix which catches our attention more quickly than the less glamorous idea of developing monitoring systems to guarantee arms reduction treaties or trying to work for peace with a people who live across the globe from us. Both Star Wars and Cola Wars are served up to us by the news establishment in such a way we aren't asked for input, only to take sides.

Nothing is more interest-catching than a war or a contest. We can root for our favorites and develop emotional rationale for our side much as we do watching a sports contest where, to begin with, we haven't a sound basis for a preference of players.

The wars in Central America are reported and discussed almost exclusively in terms of "Contras vs. Sandinistas," "Salvadoran Army vs. Guerrillas." Maybe they should be discussed in terms of bananas, coffee and tobacco, exports and debts, doctors and teachers. To understand the true needs for peace, we need well written histories and extensive first person accounts, knowledge of geography and of earth and agricultural sciences. We have got to approach the news from a more holistic viewpoint.

In the Philippines we are brought to attention by a potential revolution—"Is Marcos going to fall or stand?"—while the critical ingredients of a stable country are beyond our ken. The American ambassador to the Philippines issued a statement to the effect that the unrest there is underlain by "a general desire for fairness," a statement which one fears will be forgotten as news from the Philippines is tailored to market ads: "Marcos vs. the Communists."

To break the habit of passive news listening, we need to believe more in our status as planetary citizens with a whole world to understand. We need to demand more from the establishment and give more of our attention to a concept of events as rooted in elemental realities of nature and shaped by complicated human histories.

—*November 14, 1985*

WAR & PEACE

Liz in Costa Rica.

A Life at Treeline:

WAR & PEACE

*In contrast to many other political move-
ments, the movement to bring peace and
sanity and mutual respect to the world
cannot succeed through any devious routes
or questionable power plays. When words
seem to fail, it [the movement] cannot turn
to weapons or acts of destruction to make its
point. The belief that peace is possible has to
be based on the very finest behaviors of
mankind.*

—March 1986

It is not easy to write about a commit-ment to peace with-out being confronted by intensely challenging points of view.

The questioning has gone on and on

Chances are you remember a favorite essay topic that one of your teachers slipped you in the course of your education. At first it looked like such a simple assignment. As soon as you attempted it, it became difficult.

It's the old, "Here I stand" or "Why I am special" essay. "Write about yourself," your teacher said lightly. "What do you value in yourself, where do your values come from? Who are you?"

You look forward to mouthing off about yourself, but you sit down to write, and you are confronted by a vast emptiness. Your mind goes too far, one step beyond the obvious answers—name, date of birth, recognized peculiarities, etc. You are something large or small, important or insignificant, unique or common. The assignment becomes a hopeless tangle of stringy cheese.

I posed a question for myself recently and found myself plunged into a similar tangle. It had to do with "working for peace." How, or why, should one work for peace in this day and age, I started by asking.

The topic offered some simple answers. Peace is good. Peace is definitely preferable to war. Peace is a product of sane people striving to unify the world family, for their own sakes and for the world's children.

I went one step too far, however, over the edge into asking, if peace is so fine, why does war appear to be a necessity? We rely on it heavily for entertainment, pride, intellectual and economic stimulation. Consider, for example, the GI Joe toys, the retelling of D-Day stories, the war games and fascination for military history, the force of weapon manufacturing to turn industrial cogs. I actually can't help asking myself if there isn't something in war—why else would it get so much air time?

Secondly, I am confounded by the argument that military strength is essential to the maintenance of democracy. Frankly, I believe democracy lives in the dignity of man, every man; and that the horror of war is not just that men are killed and mutilated, but that they become killers and mutilators of other men as dignified and worthy of democracy as themselves.

I am not sure that a democracy can be supported externally by arms when this individual dignity is not deeply considered by every one of its members. I see our democratic institutions threatened from within when military strength, mustered in the name of democracy, is used to support oligarchies and dictatorships, as I believe it is being used in Central and South America today.

It is not easy to write about a commitment to peace without being confronted by intensely challenging points of view. It occurred to me that if I posed the question to others, it might generate some deeper thinking on the subject, a probing beneath the easy assumptions that we need arms to defend democracy or that peace is good. That deeper probing was, I believe, the subtle intention of our teachers when they asked us to write about "Who I am" or "Here I stand."

What about peace? What about arms? What responsibilities do we bear as individuals for our country's development and use of arms around the world? How does our military budget affect our concepts of the dignity of man, or relate to our religious beliefs?

I finished that essay I wrote about "Here I stand." I turned it in. I wasn't entirely satisfied with my answers, and the questioning has gone on and on.

—November 30, 1984

With anniversaries of any sort there is, ideally, an opening of the diaphragm on our vision of ourselves.

Belittling observation misses the point

In letters to the editor and in regular columns, many Americans objected to observances of the fortieth anniversary of the dropping of the atom bomb on Hiroshima, Japan. Their arguments were that nothing distinguished this act of war from atrocious acts of war committed by "the other side." Their arguments also reiterated the belief that using atomic bombs on Hiroshima and Nagasaki was a necessary deterrent to further warring and the loss of many more American lives.

I think those who objected had genuine concerns about the potential one-sidedness of viewing war guilt. But I think they were wrong to belittle any observance that would bring to light the destructiveness of man's escalating weaponry.

With anniversaries of any sort there is, ideally, an opening of the diaphragm on our vision of ourselves. We let in more light on our human predicament and see greater and more accurate detail. We increase our potential to grasp the truth. Even the letters that objected to the special events surrounding Hiroshima day were part of this process.

For myself three frames of reference stand out from the picture that was recalled of the bombing of Hiroshima. On August 6, Boulder Professor David Hawkins was the guest on radio station KGNU's midday interview program. Hawkins was at Los Alamos when the atom bomb was developed. He was, at that time, the official historian of the project, and his recollections were factual and to the point. He explained that the U.S. government actually could have waited a matter of weeks to see if the Japanese were going to surrender, before it was necessary either to drop the bomb or mount an invasion. The necessity of this enormous violence, in dropping the first atom bomb, may still be argued. But I wonder if elements of human impatience and retribution weren't a part of the decision to wreak havoc.

On radio and TV I heard little about the after-effects of radiation in Japan, but this area was covered eloquently and with deep human sympathy by John Hersey in a 1985 article titled "Hiroshima," as was the book he wrote decades ago.

He wrote about individuals who suffered— "a pattern of ailments which might or might not have been attributable to the bomb: liver dysfunction, night sweats and morning fevers, borderline angina, blood spots on her legs and signs in blood tests of a rheumatoid factor." Radiation sickness included weeks of high fever and periods of inexplicable fatigue. Some victims developed facial "keloids," which are, according to my dictionary, "fibrous tumors forming irregular, clawlike excrescences on the skin." The Hibakusha, or survivors of the bomb, were stigmatized in many ways.

Thirdly and finally, a small discussion took place in my own mind on August 6 when considering whether or not to count the small children who participated in "Pause for Peace" with members of the Mountain Forum for Peace. It didn't take me long to conclude they were worth counting, not because their future is at stake in how we view the dropping of the first atomic bomb, but because their hearts and minds are, I believe, truly aligned against any repetition of the deed, being less prone to complicated rationalizations than we are as adults.

—*August 22, 1985*

Expediency rules the day, and we are all the poorer for it.

We're building shelters for what?

We had a sculpture dedication in Nederland over the weekend. The area around the peace garden was flooded with people. I had the feeling of a bonding of community in support of the idea of peace and reconciliation. The spirit behind the sculpted moment of peace between two races of North American inhabitants seemed to run through us, and we took pride in what community can do.

Conversely, it often seems to me that we retreat to our own fiefdoms and are separate from each other on matters of serious import. We focus on our jobs, family, friends, property and survival in a cutthroat capitalistic world, and rely too heavily on representative democracy to achieve our common goals. Congress is assigned the task of marshaling the economic power of the people for the common good. One "good" we may all be participating in, in the fiscal years to come, is building shelters: nice, climate controlled shelters, big as gymnasiums, at approximately $105 million each.

These taxpayer-funded structures aren't for people, however. They are for bombers. It seems that little boondoggle, the B-2, is sensitive to weather. B-2 stands for $2 billion each, stands for stealth. Stealth qualities to evade radar apparently are water soluble. Each $2 billion bomber that's been built to date requires a climate-controlled hangar to protect its sophisticated outer skin and to prevent storm water from puddling in sensitive places.

The B-2 bomber is a long story, with chapters practical, political, social and environmental. In the face of much opposition, Congress voted in favor of the bombers, delivering a $44.7 billion contract to Northrup Grumman Corporation, which has built 14 of the planned 21 planes—of which eight are currently air-worthy. Lucky Northrup Grumman! This business of keeping military contractors afloat seems to influence the already slouching moral stance of many of our politicians.

President Clinton has lifted a ban on arms sales to Latin American countries that has been in effect since Jimmy Carter's presidency. Clinton didn't want to see American arms makers held out of a profitable market. This does not involve taxpayers dollars directly, but it is a situation in which we are unwilling support for our government's lack of principle. Expediency rules the day, and we are all the poorer for it. Lifting the arms ban spreads the contagion of using community resources for things, not people, or for only a select portion of the population.

Many Latin American leaders have decried Clinton's decision to lift the sales ban. They don't want to see their countries' resources channeled into a hemispheric arms race, shoving aside education, sustainable economic development, health care programs and yes, sometimes, shelter for the poor. In another example of the primacy of arms sales driving policy, consider an expanded NATO in the light of pressure on newly admitted eastern European countries to buy more sophisticated weaponry.

The investment in the high-tech world where aerospace and military expenditures intersect has two serious side effects. It is delaminating society, separating those who profit from those with genuine needs. A whole and wholesome society would want to provide for these needs. Secondly, the military-industrial complex is indifferent to environmental costs of its production. The words 'conservation' or 'sustainability' aren't in its vocabulary.

So many tender things are exposed to the weather; a whole world of children survives without homes. Yet, U.S. taxpayers—some so prosperous, so preposterously naive—will pay taxes to shelter instruments of war.

—August 28, 1997

War has been an easier alternative for centuries.

What then is for us?

On the first full day of war, I woke up to the sound of the TV and the flickering square of images reflected in a window. It was pathetically early in the morning, I thought, and my sleep had been disturbed by news the night before of air strikes beginning against Iraq.

Not being an entirely optimistic person, I struggle to start each day brightly. This morning the drone of male voices sounding self-absorbed, the enumeration of weaponry like a pre-game analysis of football players, was challenging me more than usual. I looked out a near window to the stars, and saw a plane pass through the sky, reminding me of the strange airships in my dreams. I pulled the covers over my head, and repeated to myself my own words about courage, faith and grief. Courage, yes, even as I huddled under the covers: a courage to believe in alternatives to war.

Then the TV was off, and I could get up. But while I have the privilege of turning war off with the twist of a dial, others are not so fortunate. In spite of clean talk of "strikes," "sorties" and installations, I know in another part of the world people are suffering pain and fear and death, while a landscape is pulverized—land that has nurtured another culture: music, food, symbols and philosophies budding and twining up from it.

Desert Shield has turned into Desert Storm, though I keep thinking Desert Sword. Would that have been a better name for this show? In any case, the TV producers have outdone themselves with previews that would do the theaters proud. and theater it is: the Persian Gulf theater—rated PG by the Pentagon. Not for our immediate consumption the tidal wave of fear that can make one crap his pants, nor the pain of being hit, nor the smoke of burning oil fields blotting out the sun.

What is for us, then? The agony of stricken families, the haunting faces of the captured, the letters from service men who are growing up fast, opening their hearts in some directions they've never opened them before, closing them in others.

At home, people who could be friends are viewing each other with suspicion: are you for it or against it? We each seem to have a high stake in our positions. For myself, I see the U.S. defining itself more blatantly as a warrior nation with right on its side, setting up and knocking down dictators; this is not the definition that I want to be part of. The argument that Saddam Hussein had to be stopped, that there was no other course of action, obliterates too many contradictory truths, including the argument that sanctions (not kind) would have worked in concert with the cumulative war-weariness of the Iraqi people. The insistence that we had to meet naked aggression denies our own history of aggressions in low intensity conflicts that have resulted in hundreds of thousands of dead around the world—unnamed wars that have allied us with brutal dictators.

Assuming we get past this one, how often will we be called on to perform the duty of military chastisement, plunging even further into debt and ignoring issues like global warming, racism and energy dependency? When will we be able to include those who work for health, peace and education, who practice conservation, as patriots? War has been an easier alternative for centuries. And for the moment we still have the luxury of listening to the wind in open skies, of watching sunrises, sunsets and evenings full of stars, without the awful fear that something will rain down from them.

—January 24, 1991

We also need to jolt the media out of their Pavlovian vibrations with the public.

Post-war celebrations miss points

How does it feel to have protested the war and now to witness the sense of vindication that many people feel and the glowing optimism that the United States can "get the job done," as some would have it? I have no problem giving thanks for the small numbers of American lives that were lost, nor feeling relief with families who know their close ones are safe, nor rejoicing that our bombs have stopped raining on Iraq. But my country looks no safer, no stronger to me, and I have no greater pride in it than I did before the war; my pride would be based on other things than military triumphs.

A much discussed *Boulder Daily Camera* commentary on the Buff's Orange Bowl victory comes to mind. "Now Coloradans can feel good about themselves," wrote Julie Hutchinson. Residents of the state could throw off what she characterized as "an inferiority complex."

"Because a football team won a game?!" many readers asked back. What about air and water quality, education, an informed electorate, fair taxation, well babies and other indicators of the health and greatness of our state? A football team is going to fix all that?

I haven't thought of those kinds of things first, however. What has pierced me is the ignorance or indifference we seem to feel toward the devastation in the Mideast, how little we seem to empathize with our

Iraqi brothers and sisters, or relate to the destruction of the environment and an archaeological record at the heart of our civilization. I believe we are one world and one family; most religions are built on this concept, and the basic human experience includes reverence for the earth. In the flush of victory, we have either suppressed these values and emotions, or we discover they have been bred out of us, perhaps by our excessive materialism.

We may never know how many Iraqis lost their lives in the short period of the Persian Gulf War. Secretary of Defense Dick Cheney has brushed aside the question, and the media seem indifferent to pursuing it. In Nederland, however, a memorial service will honor all the dead of this war.

After wondering what is left of broad vision and compassion, I can consider some of the other problems we face. While our stalwart president pursues wars on crime and drugs, I feel a more important concern would be to educate the American public to vote instead of waving flags—if long-term trends continue, we should have about 25 percent of our eligible voters show up for the next presidential election. Education needs to overcome the tendency to think that the United States can intervene anywhere, anytime to bring about the solutions it wants.

We also need to jolt the media out of their Pavlovian vibrations with the public. The media, which devoted a large portion of their time and space to human interest stories about families of soldiers during this war, seem content to make the public feel good, and the public seems to want nothing more. If the media deliver the information—and they might if we demand it loudly enough—we might begin to discuss the costs of this war in human lives, in dollars, in terms of environment and of the values embraced by our culture.

At the end of the war, I give thanks for one more thing: our mountain community showed the acceptance of diversity and the acceptance of protest to a greater extent than other parts of the country, where war became an excuse for "patriotism" turned rabid and ugly. I give thanks to those who agreed with me and to those who have not, most of whom have maintained sincere and supportive communications.

—March 14, 1991

AT TREELINE

Liz's Caribou cabin with her dog Girlie guarding the porch.

A Life at Treeline:

AT TREELINE

A sense of place is a nice thing to have. It's something sustaining for the individual, creating a base line of experience. With all the information that comes flying into our faces, a sense of place provides something solid that can be built and relied upon. Knowing where the sun comes up each morning is part of a sense of place, as is knowing where the moon will appear at night, or what wild berries you can chew on—if not for nutrition, at least for a little reminder of what the wild tastes like.

—January 1995

Unlock the secret of reverence for land

To be at the edge of the tundra is...a tongue into the beast, an on-ramp to a journey that justifies life...

I locked my keys in my car one summer day, in front of the Nederland post office. My only alternative seemed to be stick out my thumb, get home for a back-up key, return to unlock the door and get on with my life. That's what I did, and as is so often the case, I had an interesting time of it. I caught a ride with a man visiting this country from an Oriental city, who had rented a car and was out for a scenic drive. "What's that up there?" he asked, pointing at the tundra. "Is that just dirt?"

It seemed so important to convey that tundra was dirt raised to the nth degree of beauty, into a multitude of hardy plants, clever in their survival above timberline, a surface like no other on the land, something called tundra, a place where the spirit could rise so far above the concept of dirt and still remain rooted in it.

I like to hike up there and roll in it, literally and figuratively. To be at the edge of the tundra is a potent feature in my dream landscape as well as in my waking hours. It's a tongue into the beast, an on-ramp to a journey that justifies life in a way that earning a fortune, or winning the lottery, could never do. It is to rise above the material gratifications and to sink below the chit-chat of everyday consciousness. I hold memories from the tundra that are as precious as children to me— memories of breaking loose from the sediment of daily life to be engulfed in clouds of moths dancing on the wind, marbling the sky, or to lie in a depression where the grasses grow deep, watching butterflies perform like Botticelli.

The peaks rising steely-hard out of the tundra march, dance, play hide-and-seek, rear up like beasts, like gods, or fade into damp veils of cloud, while below one's eyes, forests run down to highways, plains, valleys and towns. Sometimes the tundra is covered in sunflower yellow, sometimes matted in forget-me-not blue. Sometimes it is clumped with succulent red leaves turned from green by early fall dips of the temperature. Kestrels play leap-frog over the ridges or hover like hummingbirds above fruitful fields of small, mammalian activity. Eagles cross the sky, only slightly lower than the rumbling jets.

Dirt, you ask, Dirt?! Up there, what looks so monotonous from the highway, are rocks the colors of jade and ruby, or pink as flesh, grey like pewter, black as oil. On them are lichens spattered like cake decorations. Where large rocks have fallen together in a stable concatenation of stone, lichen, bird droppings and acid stains of pika piss, you can only wonder about the mysterious openings into another world, guarded by fat spiders trembling on their webs.

And even those of us who know that tundra is something more than dirt might fail at times to appreciate the shifting patterns of fell-fields, soil depressions full of black-fringed sage, patterned ground, wet sinks lined by fertile silt, of grasses and cushion plants. Walk two or three feet and you are in another plant community— another neighborhood. Butterflies love it there, and you know, butterflies are often called upon to represent the soul.

—November 14, 1996

When do we recognize the cumulative impacts of our species on the ecosystem and where do we back off?

Not all trails are good (or bad)

What I love about hiking on mountain trails, or mountain biking on country roads, is that it's a time to see things. Working my way under my own power, my eyes are open. So is my mind. Many trail advocates seem to be wearing blinkers, however. They see the goodness of their recreational desires and seem not to see the issues involved in trail proliferation or overuse. We all gotta have what we gotta have.

The trail debate is raging in Colorado. The state, so attractive recreationally, is being inundated by people. Sheer numbers using existing trails and spreading out on new trails, while other open land is lost to private development, is part of a larger ecological crisis. If we are to deal with it, we all need open eyes.

Boulder County's trail debate first hit the papers when land managers attempted to close the Bobolink trail along the banks of South Boulder Creek, where it runs out of the mountains and onto the plains. They had observed river bank erosion, the wearing away of plant cover and the loss of native plant species. Further studies showed the absence of bird species that ordinarily inhabit the lusher realm of riverside habitat. Trail users were unwilling to back off use of the trail. People are part of the ecosystem, too, and people need trails, they declared.

When I look at the obvious impact of people on the ecosystem, it seems to me we could be more circumspect about how much we demand from all areas: housing, transportation routes, power generation and transmission, water storage and movement, and recreation. When do we recognize the cumulative impacts of our species on the ecosystem and where do we back off?

Another controversial trail, the Continental Divide National Trail, has its enthusiastic supporters (press releases claiming the trail is a great protector of the environment pass my desk almost every week). Environmental groups are disappointed, however, by recent Forest Service approval of a mostly tundra-alignment for the trail from Rollins Pass to Copper Mountain. The approved route invites illegal vehicle access, they say, and they question if the Forest Service has the budget to prevent damage to tundra and delicate ecosystems.

Trail backers exalt in the idea of a completed tread from top to bottom of the country, following the physical divide as much as possible. In contrast, some of us think how much more wonderful it would be to know that portions of the great divide exist without a designated human pathway through them, silent witness to the longer process of planetary evolution. In their push to complete the trail, backers have enlisted corporate sponsors—their logos will be in evidence along the costly-to-construct national trail.

In the Magnolia Road area, some trail users seem to argue that any trail is fair game for mountain biking, whether it was originally an elk trail, a rutted mining road or an illegally-cut tread, created without a public process to assess potential damage to the land. I hope a public process will prevail and that we will recognize the need for compromise, both to provide for a legitimate recreational use and to protect what is so great a treasure: land functioning as a healthy system, its vibrant fabric intact, providing home for the biodiversity that ultimately supports human life.

Aldo Leopold wrote of the dangers of a "merely economic" attitude toward the land. The conservation ethic he helped to promote has created some protection of public lands from economic exploitation. Now, we need to beware of a merely recreational view of the land with its own destructive consequences.

—*September 18, 1997*

The canyon holds us in a special embrace between the over-crowded plains and the claus-trophobic familiarity of home.

Boulder Canyon: a gorgeous drive

From the highway, the ice climbers in upper Boulder Canyon are tiny figures on a frozen waterfall. The scene reminds me of the Chinese scrolls that inspired Gary Snyder's poem, "Mountains and Rivers without End," where the ink brush brings mountains, trees, rivers and coastlines to life in bold swirls, while the eye must search out the small images of men—on trails, in boats.

This proportion of man to nature is forgotten to us most of the time, but that's something I love about Boulder Canyon. You can still find it there.

The temptation is to look at Boulder Canyon and detail the human history that marks its sides. Another way of viewing it is for itself, starting with the movements of earth and water. The walls of the canyon from the drop below Barker Dam to the exit near Settler's Park are granite, though at that point granite gives way to sandstone on the surface of the earth.

That old granite, dating back to earth's earliest eras, is pink and grey and tinged with green, reflecting in an eerie way the colors of the liquid that has carved it. Cuts in the canyon walls show the clean granite colors, unstained by time: madras colors, watercolor washes that could stain the sides of a fish.

Boulder Canyon is a trip. I like to drive it slowly enough to enjoy its wild manifestations, though I'm smart enough not to hold up long lines of traffic. I like to take in the deciduous shrubs and trees that rim the river: the dark lace of river birches, the golden wands of willows, the pale and slender arch of aspen and mountain cottonwoods that nurtures the myths of young women turned to trees. The barren winter trunks and branches remind me of underwater coral; they quiver with receptive life in the currents of the canyon air.

The water flow in the river is altered by man. Above Boulder Falls, the river is almost dry, its nourishing flow blocked by Barker Reservoir. Below the Public Service hydro-electric plant, near the tunnel, a line of white ice marks high water from the daily releases to generate electricity.

The creek (Middle Boulder) is a dividing line between two regimes: sun and shade, a southern and northern cast to the vegetation and animal life. On the north side, dark Douglas firs hug the canyon walls. On the south side, especially at lower elevations, dryland mountain junipers share terrain with ponderosa pines.

The steep south-facing walls above Boulder Falls harbor rare ferns and lichens that I can only imagine from my car. I love the aprons of boulders that pour down towards the creek—the motion of flowing rock stopped by time, that almost magical "angle of repose," where rock and soil stop sliding and hold firm. When I am driving up the canyon, the burnt ridge where the Black Tiger fire ran its course looms stark with snow, like a peak on the Divide.

The canyon has a dramatic tension posed by contradicting forces—the motion of time and the immovability of rock, a liquid effervescence versus a granite solidity. One works on the other; together, the whole is more than the parts. And we, in our hard metal shells atop turning wheels, confined to asphalt bounded by artificial banks of sand, pass through this beauty, possessing it only as a brief mental image.

The road is a corridor through living fabric in which we cling to our music, our audio tapes, we grab with our eyes, sometimes we stop to savor briefly the awesome nature. The canyon holds us in a special embrace between the overcrowded plains and the claustrophobic familiarity of home. At times, if we're lucky, it makes us feel small.

—*January 23, 1997*

We are destroying places with the mistaken sense that every place should be accessible to us at a moment's notice.

Colorado bicycling in the 1940s

As Catherine drove the car from Carbondale to Aspen, my father told us of a trip he had taken over the same territory in the 1940s. He had taken his bicycle, an English three-speed, on a train called either the Prospector or the Mountaineer, from Denver to Glenwood Springs— there were two trains at that time that ran west into the mountains.

From Glenwood Springs, he caught a freight train servicing the mining and agricultural community of the Roaring Fork valley, to Aspen. Aspen, of course, was a mouldering mining town—no hint of the ski culture that possesses it today.

From Aspen, he rode his bike over Independence Pass, camping along the way to reach the Gore Range and scramble up a few summits, some of which, he recalled, might have been first ascents since there was no indication anyone else had ever been on them. He finished the week-long journey near Long's Peak campground, rejoining my mother, my young brothers and I, in a small cabin there. In fairness, I report that he took care of us at times when she had work or adventures to follow.

As Dad told the story, I looked out the window of the car to a scene that was once the epitome of mountain splendor—a fertile river valley surrounded by aspen and pine-cloaked hills reaching up to snow-capped peaks. These days it's more analogous to any long boulevard on the outskirts of Denver, Albuquerque or Santa Fe; four busy lanes of traffic interrupted by construction and lights, with cars occupied by a single person leap-frogging one another in the rush to work or pleasure. The valley and hillsides are crusted with homes and businesses; the emphasis is on getting somewhere else, rather than enjoying and protecting what is there.

The corridor between Aspen and towns to the north of it is equivalent to the corridor we are creating between Boulder and Nederland. Looking at Colorado's landscape overall, not even the making of plutonium war heads has been as disfiguring as highway building. Mining, milling, logging and ranching pale in comparison as extractive and destructive activities.

We are destroying places with the mistaken sense that every place should be accessible to us at a moment's notice. Our government and public servants, from President Clinton to Nederland's town board, demonstrate ignorance and lack of foresight in not seeking out alternatives. So-called leaders continue to promote landscape defilements that produce nothing but a slew of pollutants.

Some alternatives to increasing the volume of vehicles traveling between Boulder and Nederland are to provide for public transportation that works for more people. Nederland can also reduce dependence on automobile tourism—at least the in-out, quick trip, passing-through type—by providing more places for visitors to rest and explore.

Individually, we can establish transportation budgets that minimize the amount of driving we must do. Ironically, our choice to live in the mountains in spread-out development creates new congestion and requires us to spend more time in traffic on the road.

My father came here because of his love for the mountains. He came intending them no harm. At 80, he still walks and rides the bus to get around in Boulder, more days than he drives.

—*July 1, 1993*

The climb
up the
mountain
would have
been mildly
agonizing
as a recre-
ational
venture, but
was effort-
less, given
our purpose.

Mountain search had its price

Twenty-four hours after leaving the trailhead to search for climbing fatalities on South Arapahoe Peak, I was shocked to feel my immunity to weakness dissolving. My sunburned face felt bruised, my muscles started to tremble and I had a heaviness in my heart I couldn't redeem for any value.

I imagined I was sharing a family experience, as both my father and husband have been members of Rocky Mountain Rescue Group, which is often called in such emergencies. Many years ago the phone would ring in our new Boulder home, my father would listen intently, soon be dressed for climbing and out the door shouldering his pack, responding to anything from an alpine plane crash to a climbing accident in the canyon. Later, when he was home organizing his gear, he might mention details in a deceptively light tone, or warn about safety in a voice that broached no argument.

As I kicked steps in hard snow across the avalanche chute on an approaching ridge to South Arapahoe, I remembered being taken to summer snowbanks to practice glissading and ice-ax and self-arrests. The mountain club outings of my childhood were imbued with practicality, emphasizing technique, equipment and good judgment. As we gained altitude, I thought of my father's pack that has, even in summer, an extra pair of socks in it, mittens, a sweater and jacket, and a bag full of indestructible but calorie-rich food.

Like most training in my life, a lot flowed past me unabsorbed, but what remained was in service on Saturday's search, as I followed my husband into the area. I felt with certainty the placement of each foot as we headed up steep ravines of rock and snow. Only when I was plodding through new drifts or on relatively sure, dry ground, did I have time to look up at the rock pinnacles above me, still frosted from the sheets of blowing snow that had raged against them the night before, or have time to watch the search helicopter hovering in streams of wind, the pilot using his ship's shadow as a pointer to possible footprints on the mountain's snowy flank.

Sometimes a gust would press us against the ladder steps of loose rock, ice and snow. Then a lull would change the environment: for an instant the air would be warm and the mountain seem beneficent. I listened to the radio clatter building information bit by bit, as clues led searchers to the victims.

The climb up the mountain would have been mildly agonizing as a recreational venture, but was effortless, given our purpose. I scarcely heard the ripping sound of wind around us, and only occasionally stopped to admire the magnificence of snow and granite that cradled us, making me feel small and great, all at once. Then I'd notice exquisite corniced ridges across the valley that seemed translucent at the edges, contrasting with the profound darkness of bare rock. Under foot were ice lenses over lichen-spotted rock, across the valley ice shimmered on sheer faces. Carefully guarded in one corner of my mind was the image of the victims as grains of chaff slapped down by the mountain's enormity.

I felt privileged to share the drama of finding them. But privilege has its price, and the following day I had to grapple with sadness that was hard to localize. I couldn't be sad for the bodies, because they were clearly beyond suffering. But I felt a dull anger that, though I'd never know them, the young people weren't out there in the mass of humanity somewhere, exciting the imagination of those who were close to them and feeling for themselves the busy flutter of life. I didn't think it was my job to cry for them; my job had been the simple task of using my mountain sense to help to find them.

But finally I had to cry for them as though they were my own, to imagine rocking them and soothing the terror they must have known, trying to reassure them that they were loved, in life and in death, however indifferent we may have seemed when we came out of the field discussing footgear and energy foods. I had to cry for them, hurting strangely because there were no recollections of the living to bring me joy, and no one to tell that they were in a place of beauty, in an equation of such complexity that their mistakes were a small part of their fate.

—*June 7, 1990*

*Details to
the house
and yard
are works of
art, while
everything
conspires
to look
effortlessly
achieved.*

Small home design takes years

L ast week a county commissioners' agenda crossed my desk. One item, highlighted for my interest, is an 11,650-square-foot residence, up for site review. The planned home is not in our immediate area of coverage, it's just a prod to wonder: Who would need such a home? Who would plan such a home in the face of what we know today of the heavy weight of humans on the Earth? Extenuating circumstances? Perhaps phantoms from the last century are planning to move in: a devout Mormon family consisting of husband, a half-dozen wives and at least a dozen children. They *might* need 11,000 square feet.

Is it a black hole gobbling up limited resources? Do the people who live there find sustenance within its walls, or do they clog our highway with numerous daily car trips? Does the house itself create a need for lavish entertainment to justify its palatial rooms? What are its utility bills?

Given today's small families, such a large residence seems to stand simply to declare wealth or to conform to some imagined standard of respectable living. Different strokes for different folks, a reader might say, deflecting value judgments about house size. In this column, I am not out to condemn, but to contrast, having in the same week visited a home newly built on a beautiful piece of mountain land.

The new residence is thoroughly lived in by a family of three. Though under 1,200 square feet (one-tenth the size of the aforementioned mansion), it provides a home work space for a computer-based business and shop space as well. The living space, including kitchen, feels open and uncongested. Details of the house and yard are works of art, while everything conspires to look effortlessly achieved. It hints of Japanese lightness and elegance. In one small room, a wall of mirrors extends the feeling of space.

I noted the polished granite kitchen counter top. Above it, a large pot hanger also holds light fixtures. An ultra-efficient refrigerator is nestled into a corner so it seems to take up no space at all. I know that while costs were watched closely, certain expenditures, like the refrigerator, high-efficiency fixtures and the granite top, were made with an eye to conservation and low maintenance. Trays, drawers, shelves for storage fit under beds, stairs, and any space that isn't functioning artistically as open space. Everything is hand-built, including the finish work and hand-in-glove fixtures that make such a small space serve for three. I was impressed by the fact that just working out the basic floor plan took as much as a year, trying out one thing and then another, mulling over its usefulness.

Needless to say, it incorporates elements of solar heating and other energy-saving measures. It is so efficient, in fact, that Public Service Company turned it down for a company-sponsored grant providing solar electric panels. It didn't consume enough electricity to be a good example for the average customer! Water conservation includes rain water collection to back up well-water supplies. Nonetheless, the bathroom has a luxurious feeling to it—a deep tub (recycled) and a view.

This home took much more than a year or two to build, in fact. It stands as more than a physical accomplishment. It is the outcome of a commitment to sustainable living. Its creator got to the point of skill and financial ability, not only by studying construction and engineering principles, but understanding and being willing to work with the real estate market, the regulatory structure, and to a some extent, the fabric of society itself. The accomplishment is so idiosyncratic, so tailored to a small family's needs, so self-effacing in the conservation of resources, that it is hardly noticed. We still reward the big, the obvious, the immediate with our praise. Too bad.

—*September 4, 1997*

In my binoculars, his black cap looked as glossy as a scholar's mortar-board...He brings distant parts of the globe together in one place.

Bird count helps define ecosystems

The human tendency to build often is based on the misconception that one puts a house, a business or new rock shelter in an unspoiled location because, otherwise, nothing is there. The land is treated like indoor-outdoor carpet—to be rolled back for the dance. Land doesn't return to its former shape easily, however, and many things that were there before cannot return.

I used counting birds for a seasonal estimate of mountain populations as a device to get beneath this vision of the land. Last weekend I went out by myself, with a circle route up to the tundra in mind and unlimited time to complete it. I wanted to record as many different kinds of birds and as many individuals as possible for the "breeding" period of the Indian Peaks Bird Count. The numerical tally was not as important as feeling involved with the land and enjoying all observations that came my way.

The day illustrated the meaning of ecosystems to me. An ecosystem is defined as the interrelationship between species and their habitat. Applying this to the 200-plus bird species that have been sighted in the bird count area, an ecosystem is as large as the hemisphere, as small as willow shrub.

I saw a tiny yellow Wilson's warbler on the frost-burnt tip of a krummholz tree. In my binoculars, his black cap looked as glossy as a scholar's mortarboard. He may have flown to the rugged hillside from forests south of Mexico City. He brings distant parts of the globe together as one place. He also reminds us of the precarious existence of species that may travel far, only to find that their destination of willows or wetlands has been destroyed.

The birds I saw were for the most part forest species, though I counted a pair of horned larks grazing insects from a broad snowbank and a rock wren piping and bobbing in the rocky meadow where I have found him, or someone like him, several times before.

Mountain bluebirds fly over the krummholz islands. They nest in the smooth golden, barkless trunks of large limber pines that have neat holes the size of narrow-mouth jar lids drilled into them. Many birds seem to love the high meadows and ecozone between the tundra and dense forest. Small hawks swooped silently away from me. The new blueberry cover reminded me of a fall when the meadow was full of feasting ravens.

Mountain birds illustrate the concept of ecosystem structure, as well. The jigsaw puzzle of different forest types—aspen, lodgepole, limber and spruce-fir—offer a variety of textures and spaces. Some birds—Audubon's warblers and ruby-crowned kinglets, for example—flit and sing under the cover of pine branches. Others, like the olive-sided flycatcher, sit upright at the pointy top of a dead snag to make their song. Juncos trill loudly from the tops of pines, but build their nests on the ground beneath the sheltering fingers of low branches.

I am still learning to identify birds by sight and sound. My lack of expertise doesn't stop me from participating in the counts, however. I am helping to document what lives here and being drawn into a world of colorful and fragrant detail: including watermelon snow, the tiniest bouquets of alpine forget-me-nots, the fragrance of moss campion, the promise of spears of coral root orchids piercing the forest floor. When I have to spend time indoors, a splash of sound or beat of wing reminds me that the birds are alive to the beauty, when I cannot give my full attention to the land.

—*June 17, 1993*

*I hear
pine cones
falling,
birds prying
under bark,
raven wings
climbing,
footsteps in
the drive,
wind
beginning,
weather
changing.*

Jets destroy Braille of simple sounds

Sometimes, I swear, you can hear the sun hit the ground. You can hear the lichen growing on rocks and tree trunks. Now, I pray for those moments, when the planes aren't overhead, the traffic is slim on the road, and I can listen for the noises which speak for life.

Noise officials came to Boulder last week to determine how loud jets are traveling over us. "It's no louder than your telephone ringing," they said. DIA and FAA officials are quick to paint noise complaints from Boulder and the mountain area as a matter of "perception," an over-reaction to a problem that is, in their paradigm, a normal fact of life.

A telephone ring is designed to summon our attention and to rivet it until we pick up the phone. It's meant to provoke a response within a few seconds. Now, as too many of us are aware, jet noise makes just such a demand on our attention and holds it there without relief. There's no off-switch at our disposal, and hardly anyone to talk to about the problem.

It's disheartening to combat a problem in which one's personal judgment and environmental sensitivity count for nothing. It's difficult to resolve a conflict when you are told your perceptions aren't adequate to the task of defining it. My hope is that there are enough people out there who will continue to demand solutions— "multiple and partial solutions," if necessary, to a real and serious problem.

Mountain residents could be making a valuable statement about the deleterious effect of noise pollution on all members of society. We recognize the stress excessive noise causes; it sidetracks us from our business as productive human beings.

But what about this thing we label as "silence"? When my ability to listen to my surroundings is lobbed off by low-flying, outmoded, loud-engined planes, I feel like the top of my awareness, part of a spherical whole, has been taken from me. To listen to everything happening around me is to be allowed to be fully alive. I hear pine cones falling, birds prying under bark, raven wings climbing, footsteps in the drive, wind beginning, weather changing. These are acts of appreciation and acts of diagnosis. My natural surroundings are alive with sounds that are intricately woven and integral to the actual life-processes of the hillside. The tones and melodies change with day and night. There are seasonal differences, too. Right now, the squirrels are busy dropping cones from the trees to store through the winter. A deer silent in the woods stands with its ears pivoting like radar.

The snap of a twig is a cliché, but it means something. Subtle sounds are a Braille to be read with the ears. That sensitivity is scarred by the constant assault of noises "as loud as telephone ringing," as loud as a stage two jet traveling a few thousand feet above us.

Our self-reliance is a function of our senses, of our perceptions. I want to tell all of my representatives and those paid employees of my government that I have a right to protect my senses. I don't want them denigrated by a for-profit business, a transportation fix that may be quick but isn't energy efficient or resource conservative.

Since Denver International Airport opened some six months ago, my life has changed. My remote mountain home has become "fully-involved," as the fire departments say of a house in flames, in the urban excesses that have too long been ignored and imposed on unwilling members of our society. When a choice to be urban or rural could still be made, we made it. Now government should protect our choice. We're worth a lot, in the long run: we know and remember something of a natural world.

—*August 31, 1995*

You can have pavement, or you can have the stuff that mountain visits are made of.

Brainard can't take any more blacktop

What is beautiful in the Brainard Lake Valley is much more than the views of lakes and peaks. What is beautiful there, and all over the Front Range, is the intricate mosaic of nature made up of small pieces, sometimes as small as the ink-dot pattern of lichens on granite, as small as the pink, white, grey, black and green pebbles and fine sand that make up the ground surface.

A mosaic of tree islands and willows, a constantly shifting emphasis on species from spruce and fir to limber pine, from willow and birch to aspen and lodgepole, define the goodness of nature that is still present in the mountains, but under siege.

The Brainard Lake Valley is not a large valley, yet it holds many streams, seeps and glacial ponds, ridges and alpine lakes, glaciers and old growth forests. The valley is a blessing upon the Front Range, an exquisite Shangri-La—one that is too close to the Front Range urban corridor for its own good. In order to accommodate the hordes of visitors who find it an easy drive from Boulder, Denver and the plains megalopolis, the U.S. Forest Service is proposing more pavement.

You can have pavement, or you can have the stuff that mountain visits are made of. It's one or the other; you can't have both. We only pretend to care for the land, when we are willing to turn the Brainard Valley into a booming parking lot for urban visitors, many of whom need a long training before they can see and sense what this valley truly holds.

And yet, the U.S. Forest Service is proposing "to manage the area for heavy use with vehicular access during the summer and fall." The short growing season above 9,000 and 10,000 feet elevation will be a time of assault. Included in the long-range plan, the Forest Service proposes to construct a 150-space campground and, additionally, "the already-approved Redrock Lake Trailhead" for 250 vehicles. To those of us who know the area intimately, this is like holding a flea market in a cathedral.

As a child, I walked many times from Ward to Brainard Lake, or vice versa, either because the road was closed or because we did not have a car to take us in and out. Maybe the only salvation for Brainard Lake and other parts of the mountains is for people to have to get out of their cars, before they reach paradise.

Otherwise, it's paved and it's gone.

The Forest Service will argue that the people are already there, they have to be accommodated. Our rangers could as well argue that the beauty is already there, it has to be preserved. As informed and caring mountain residents, we have a duty to argue that the issue is not expansion here, expansion there, but expansion everywhere. Every piece of ground that has not been sold and developed for private profit is pressurized from the huge population growth in the area. The priority now is protection, holding the line, not increasing the capacity for visitors.

Our comments support those within the Forest Service who care about the land and want to protect it from over-use. The Forest Service could make smaller adjustments for visitors and still successfully manage the area. They could put the cost of pavement into rangers who can teach people to tread lightly, to care, to carpool and to measure their impacts.

The pressure on mountain lands, home to a mosaic of creatures as well as soils and plants, can only be relieved by deep changes. We must learn from spill-over problems that human growth sends out tidal waves of repercussions. Ultimately, it is up to each of us to put nature first in the way we live, then to expect and to demand the same reverence from government and corporations.

—*February 1, 1996*

In the other corner we have people needing more—electrical outlets multiplying like rabbits.

Outages cause outrage, but think again

Here I sit in a house rocking in the wind, plastered with snow, amongst twitching trees, and my computer up and running on the power of that wind. The wind turns our generator blades, which in turn charges the house batteries and passes through an inverter to my machine. I can be productive even though I cannot get to work safely because the roads are snow-blinded and icy.

I am not always so plush with power. Sometimes, I won't turn on my home computer because I don't have enough power in the batteries. Then, I feel hindered by our alternative energy source. I should meditate more often on Herman Melville's great pen-powered productivity of words, or my favorite contemporary essayist, Bruce Berger, who progresses from pencil and legal pad to manual typewriter to produce elegant and entertaining writing.

Tuesday's power interruption reminds me of when Public Service Company officials came to Nederland to explain what they were doing to correct economically damaging outages in the town. The conversation was ostensibly about providing reliable service. A lot of things interfere with the flow of electricity through the wires—including ice and snow loads and wind blown catastrophes. But customers who pay dearly for their watts and amps don't like to be penalized by unexpected failures.

During that discussion, I realized that companies

like PSCo are straining to provide adequate service to growing numbers of people. Not only are more homes or customers being added to the lines, sucking in power from the coal-powered plants, but rates of consumption are also growing. Throw in the fact that for-profit electrical companies are as dependent on growth-economics as homes and businesses are on 120 voltage, and you've got a contradiction in terms of sustainable living.

Double burden, double jeopardy. Businesses in Nederland do hurt when power outages come at peak business times. However, I am not sure it is a good thing for society—families, businesses, individuals, even university researchers on Niwot Ridge—to be predicating the functioning of their lives on uninterrupted electrical service, making it someone else's business entirely how that electricity is made and delivered. If we really want to enter a new age with an improved relationship to the world's ecosystems, it would be the age of responsible production and consumption of all things, including electricity.

We have PSCo on one side, making pretty good money, I imagine, over humanity's attachment to the juice, but starting to sweat over the complex engineering and capital investment of supplying it. In the other corner we have people needing more—electrical outlets multiplying like rabbits. We've allowed consumptive uses to escalate, while passively waiting for the (electric) door to open to a healthier future. Outage equals outrage, but who is responsible?

Our electrical dependence—with the earmarks of an addiction— illustrates our captivity to mass solutions, when it is within our grasp to operate efficiently and self-sufficiently on a smaller scale (Nederland Elementary School, for example, is prepared to generate its own power on a short-term basis). It's the customer and not the utility that has the ultimate responsibility.

Electricity itself is a kind of interruption, a wedge between us and our environment in a conceptual way. I've heard Indian activist Russell Means talk about how he felt living at primitive Thunder Camp in historic Sioux territory. Without electricity, he said, he felt like he'd finally grown up to be a real Indian. I believe he meant that he'd succeeded in experiencing what the lives of his elders were like, and that meant a lot to him.

—*October 31, 1996*

Avalanches happen in the real world

S—t happens, reads the bumper sticker. So do avalanches. Life skills have to do with avoiding such occurrences as much as possible. There's a life-skills class at Nederland High School, come to think of it, but I'm not sure it teaches avalanche safety alongside shopping and laundry strategies for the budding adult. Should avalanche safety courses be required for the backcountry? Should an omnipresent "they" post notices and scream warnings, with the legal stipulation that the dangers of snowslides reach every able-bodied resident of the state?

I'm sorry that Jeffrey Kolb lost his life last week in an avalanche in Boulder County's mountains, but I can't endorse the viewpoint that someone else was responsible for his fate. To place blame elsewhere robs him of the last shred of heroic possibility in life or in death. I'm relieved that his body was found and we didn't have more than one man hidden beneath this winter's snowpack. These young men always look like my kids when I see their pictures in the paper or hear about them on the news. I grieve for them, but the mistakes they made have been their own.

The last adventurer lost, in November, may turn up this spring in a shrinking snowbank. He was an inexperienced cross-country skier who set off alone at 9,000 feet at the end of a wintry afternoon with few clothes, inappropriate equipment and good intentions to sample a Colorado adventure. He met with intense winds, blinding snow, darkness, a minimally marked trail, falling temperatures and who knows what else. The Forest Service has since invested heavily in signing the area. While there, it has defaced the Sourdough trail for hiking, skiing and bicycling with over-large caution signs warning, "Bridge Ahead," for the small, tranquil Peace Bridge that crosses a minor trickle in the woods.

We may question whether or not the state should protect innocents who venture onto undeveloped public or private land for recreation. How you answer the question depends on how you view wilderness—"wilderness" in a broad sense. Is our relation to nature—its hazards, its challenges—a privilege or a right?

I argue that from birth or even conception it is as much a privilege as a right. It's a privilege to be here, especially in western Boulder County, a place of awesome beauty. It's a privilege to share the ground not only with a fascinating variety of creatures, but to find ourselves as small as fleas on the greatest of the wildlife—Gaia, planet Earth, clothed in a botanical raiment beyond our ken.

We have to pay for privilege with responsibility, not just to others of our species but to the phenomena of weather, terrain, seasons and wildlife. It's our responsibility to know what humans can do and what they can't do. Our lives should center on enlarging our survival skills, not just in the mall, marketplace or high rise, but in places like the upper Eldora Valley, where the steep walls have collected snow and metamorphosis has guaranteed its instability.

Some who responded to last week's tragedy were poorly prepared for the environment they met on the scene. They rushed there from lower elevations; they confused the requirements of city and mountain. And many expected machine transport—snow cats and helicopters taking the place of traditional oversnow travel by foot or specialized snowmobile.

With the proliferation in the county of conveniences and warnings more typical of city than of nature, both foresight and proportion are in danger of being lost. Soon, every move we make in either locale could require the direction and protection of that mysterious "they," or shall we just say, "big brother."

—March 12, 1992

204

FAMILY

Liz with her father, son Bill, daughter-in-law Diana, and new grandson.

A Life at Treeline:

FAMILY

Rubbing our noses in each other as a family makes bittersweet sense. Each of us teaches something to the other: a little common sense, humility or pride, modernity, humor, kindness and shyness, acceptance of ourselves as we are and as we want to be. These things come stronger, perhaps, through the family group— connections made, strengthened, accepted.

—February 1996

Knowing her has been one of those places in my life.

She told her stories and inspired others

Many of us write to say, "I've been there," the same way explorers plant flags and leave behind the detritus of expeditions in valleys, at poles, on summits. It's not enough for us to have lived and experienced the varied landscape of life. We want to keep alive each moment to pass on to others the breadth of our experience.

My mother-in-law, who died last week, was much better at telling stories than at writing them down, and you couldn't get her to tell her stories to order, either. The moment had to be right. Then, her voice and eyes would crackle with electricity and her thin body would take on height. Then, she had a magician's command of our attention, and her stories, that would appear rather simple when I would copy them in my journal, were as satisfying as hand-cranked ice cream licked from the beaters.

Many stories were about her experiences in Nederland and other mountain towns. She came to the Nederland area as a young woman following her husband—an engineer and miner—in the 1930s. She lived on the hill near the elementary school and down in Tungsten, which used to be more convincingly a town.

"She always let us know she was just a little smarter than the rest of us," Rosy Northrup remembers, and we imagine she did do that sometimes. She was a mover, in a hard-working, genteel Southern tradition.

The mountain life may have been a little foreign to her but always fascinating.

Rosy remembers a blizzard in 1932 or thereabouts, when she and Dorothy shared Nederland. "We were running out of groceries and this and that and waiting for days for the roads to open up. What's the first thing we saw coming round the corner at Tungsten? The beer truck!"

That was the kind of story Dorothy would tell. That and about ersatz coffee sold out of Ted Green's store during the Depression; about dancing and playing cards; about coming up the canyon with a new baby, being stopped by a rock slide that blocked the road and rescuing another couple trapped by the slide; of running to ring the fire bell in the middle of town.

I believe she was pregnant with her first child, my husband, when she and her husband spent the winter in a tent house in Lakewood—the site is east of today's entrance to Caribou Ranch. She remembered a man on horseback barging halfway into her home, through the canvas flaps of the tent, when she was alone, and how she diplomatically steered him on his drunken way. Years later, she drove to mountain schools to teach reading and remembered one crisis, a young child burnt on the pot belly stove in the Gold Hill School.

I was never quite sure what to call her—I had a "Mom," and "Dottie" seemed too familiar as we got to know each other, so I may have been one of the few who called her Dorothy. She was grateful and exhausted when she could finally address me as her daughter-in-law instead of her oldest son's "friend."

Knowing her has been one of those places in my life. She conveyed to me through her stories and photo albums and very genuine friendship some of the highlights and satisfying details of her entire 80 years. She didn't have to write them down; sharing them in good conversation was enough. To the last, she affected all who met her with her interest in other lives as well, quick as a red fox to point out the positive possibilities in everyone.

—March 15, 1990

We pay a high price for our treasured and un-examined mobility, fleeing the places and people who shaped us.

Families suffer from delamination

I ran into a childhood neighbor at a wedding recently, in the midst of other familiar Boulder faces. Fay is in her 70s, but, my son Billy and I agree, she seems not to have aged in the last 20 years, when she has with good humor seen many of us through many changes.

We were standing in one of the rooms of the University Club in Boulder, where I can remember being one of the younger set at such occasions (10 years old, flitting restlessly between the drink- and food- and conversationally-encumbered adults). Fay broke into a smile and sighed. "Oh, I wish we could go back 40 years! We all lived in the same block and there were 26 children," she told my husband, "and two of the lots didn't even have houses on them!"

The Sixth Street crowd—newcomers to a new land, our homes breaking up the prairie-clay soil at the base of the Flatirons, in the shadow of Flagstaff. Flocks of children, with so much to look forward to, so little apparently lacking in our lives. But looking back, I see we were lacking one thing on a consistent, daily level: grandparents. We were contained by the neat, nuclear American family, with other relatives in distant states.

I have to grope to remember my grandparents' names, separated from my childhood by death or the Atlantic Ocean. Few of my schoolmates had grandparents to whom they were close or large families that swallowed them up like an ocean, tranquil or storm-tossed. My generation had a distorted view of its own importance, uninformed by the tides of other family members birthing and dying. Other people aged, old people existed in the world, but our day-to-day reality was compressed into the nuclear family, and youth seemed the definite norm.

How quaint the concept of many generations in one place seemed—comparable to a nostalgic picture of family farms or the layered, immigrant communities in large cities. Now, from the same, self-centered point of view, I am awed with my own discovery of vertical layers of family. It seems a privilege, a rarity, to have as many close family members as I have, with an age range of 1 to 80-plus, on the local phone exchange.

As much as anything, I love the impromptu exchange of stories that takes place with frequent visiting. We easily go back to other times, comparing notes and rediscovering each other at different stages. Then, we return with a laugh to the present, weaving in and out of time: "Gotta go—don't forget..." I love the history written in my grandson's big, four-tooth smile, a smile that reminds me of Fay's stories of my son at the age: "He was the smartest child I've ever known!" (No wonder we're fond of Fay!)

When certain factions get out the drum and start beating a death knell for the American family, blaming single parents for its demise, I think, that's not the problem. There is so much resentment in the charge—as if single parents weren't nestled within families of their own. The American family is weakened as much by the delamination between generations as it is by the high rate of divorce or the decision to go parenting alone.

Moving away from one's parents creates a more subtle loss, complicated by the search for economic opportunity. It creates a more subtle fragmentation that affects our knowledge of history and our respect for place. We pay a high price for our treasured and unexamined mobility, fleeing the places and people who shaped us.

And Fay—how does she stay so young? Would the fact that several of her children and grandchildren live today within a stone's throw of Sixth Street have anything to do with it?

—July 28, 1994

For him, nature is there for the nourishment of the soul, and as long as the planet is healthy it will fulfill its purpose.

Thanks for the view, Dad!

Father's Day is coming up, and I thought I'd stay in the family track a little longer and write about my Dad. He has been making himself known around Nederland. He likes to come here, either driving up listening to opera in his car or by bus, for a change of scene from the busy Boulder streets he's known for over 40 years.

He likes to go to Whistler's Restaurant, where he's made to feel at home, and to patronize a variety of other local businesses.

"Dad, you romanticize Nederland," I tell him. "I suppose I do," he replies. "But I like it, and I would enjoy the challenge of living up here if I ever retire." At 76, he is still teaching, writing and researching.

My Dad has shown me a lot of things over the years and many admirable approaches to life. But when I began exploring my thoughts about him for a column, one thing stood out—a little hard to pin down in words.

My Dad is probably responsible for what feels like an eccentric behavior in me: I see nature from the outside in. Most of us see nature from the inside out, I think, as though it is an asterisk to our existence. I prefer to feel as though I am an asterisk on nature's pages, a momentary blip on its screen.

Sure, I like the comfort of a warm home or car and the companionship of friends. But to be happy, I have to get away from these things fairly often, to feel part of the larger reality beyond those human boundaries.

Dad might have something to do with this. Before I was a teenager, he had taken me up Long's Peak and a half-dozen other Front Range mountains. He'd had the patience to lead me up the face of one of Boulder's Flatirons. He'd taken me to distant peaks with the Colorado Mountain Club and backpacking with the rest of the family in Idaho, Montana and Canada.

My adult life has been punctuated by our all-day outings, when we've achieved summits I never would have persevered to alone. Even now I let him set the pace. I walk behind him, usually in silence. We sometimes lose the trail and see the country from unmarked points. And in the process of our exertions, I become absorbed by the land around me and feel inside of what is usually referred to as outside.

The silence of our being together contributes to this process. But my experience also grows from an attitude my father has of not needing to hold in his possession either summit victories or tracts of mountain land. For him, nature is there for the nourishment of the soul, and as long as the planet is healthy it will fulfill its purpose. There is little compulsion or anxiety to his love for it. His relationship to it has taught me a faith and admiration for nature that has tunneled to my core.

My Dad and I don't always see eye to eye, and my observations in nature are often different than his. But I think I can lay a baseline of my perception at his door, with thanks, and commend him to the town of Nederland. If he brings this perspective to the town, it will benefit all.

—June 16, 1988

It's a practice fall—too soon, too fast, but would I ever take it in my stride?

Keeping my son on a tight rope

Something twitches at the edge of my vision—a slither the color of the volcanic rock but of indeterminate size. For an instant I am electrified by the imagined conflict of a snake coiled behind me and my responsibility to hold the rope that runs through my hands and coils at my feet.

"Hey, look!" my son calls cheerfully from the vertical face, fifteen feet above me, nodding with his head, and I realize it's a small lizard, like others I've watched skittering across the dark basalt, secure without belay.

The canyon is quiet, except for the piercing calls of wrens who posture at its upper edges and the mid-flight quarrels of the swallows whose nests are daubed urn-like under lips of stone. Now and then a train rumbles by unseen, the weight of its cars shaking the rails penetrating phantom-like into this subsurface world. The canyon opens to a mix of blue New Mexico sky and up-swirling summer clouds, as I steadily pull the rope down, careful never to disengage my braking hand, the hand that will hold my son if he falls.

Earlier, drifts of sound came round the corner from two young climbers: rumbles of scree, the gentle commands of "climbing," "on-" and "off belay," discussions of their routes. They greeted us politely, but we must have been an odd pair, I thought, Dan, an able climber, and I, without dispute, his mother. Well, I've done this before, I thought, but never like this—protecting my youngest son, top-roped by means of an anchor he has painstakingly set with bright nylon slings.

"You know what you're doing?" I asked him once; when he's on the rock, it's no time to overdo the parental role. I was the student as he clipped my climbing harness into another anchor and showed me how the rope goes around the "eight," a piece of hardware designed to hold the rope by friction, clipped to my harness by two opposing carabiners. This arrangement, and the intricacies of the knot he's tied around his climbing harness, are spatial problems I am slow in solving, so I let him solve them for me and concentrate on the principle of the brake.

He checks on my technique for taking up rope and giving slack. "Fast learner, Mom," he declares. He's on the rock like a lizard, appendages spread out, holding, advancing, and then—"I'm going to fall."

It's a practice fall—too soon, too fast, but would I ever take it in my stride? I hold him, but tremble at the cushiony elastic of the rope; my heart is beating faster. It is beautiful to watch him climb, to comprehend first the ease and then the effort as he overcomes a difficult stretch with a complex play of muscles, will power and measured breath.

When he's tired himself out on the sixty-foot walls, I poke while he cleans up his anchors and packs his gear. The midday sun glares into the canyon. The vegetation is strange to me, though I recognize tamarisk and willow. Muddy pools are still and reflective. Brush and driftwood are caught six to ten feet above the bottom of the wash, telling me it must run with tremendous volume after rains fall hard over the land above us.

I'm ready to go, but wait for Dan to look at fish hanging in the water in a crack of shade thrown by a large boulder. We've been too close, connected by the rope, for me to complain, but I remember that he is the child who has always been magnetized by water and who can spend hours looking, probing, catching. The sun beats down. I am his slave, though later he will drive and cook for me, and hold me tight before I board my plane. And I have held him on the rope and felt the tension in my life soar up in a constructive spiral.

—June 20, 1991

The two
young
men are
learning to
negotiate a
wide world
that can be
dangerous,
a world that
can take you
by surprise.

Lessons learned away from home

The phone rang at 6:30 on Saturday morning, and I went to answer it slowly, reasoning that anyone pressed to reach us at that time would let it ring for awhile. It took me a second to figure out which son was saying "Mom, it's me." Middle son, Ben, in South America. "I'm all right but Caleb's up sh-t creek. Take down this number and call me back. I've got to talk to Skip."

I hang up the phone and holler a "holy sh-t" myself. We've had more than one long-distance emergency phone call in the past week, in addition to summons for my husband's mountain rescue work close to home. Skip got on the phone to Ben, a very long-distance conference on pulmonary edema. Ben was frantic and in a hurry. More than once we called back the Bolivian home that had let Ben use the phone, to clarify details: "Continuous oxygen! Get lower! Don't roll the Jeep!" Then Ben was gone to take his friend to good medical care. It was unclear whether he had yet found oxygen for him. We waited 12 hours for the news that his traveling companion, Caleb Melamed, was in a hospital and stabilized after a near-death experience.

High altitude pulmonary edema preys on strong young men. Caleb fit the profile in Skip's old copy of *Medicine for Mountaineers,* which he had pulled off the shelf after the first call. Those who have acclimatized to the mountains, dropped down to a lower elevation (Ben and Caleb had spent almost a week at sea level in Chile), and gone back to high elevations are particularly susceptible. We learned that the boys, as we think of them, had gone above 10,000 feet and were resting one night before trekking, when Caleb felt tightening in his chest, Ben could hear gurgling in his lungs, and he was spitting out pink liquid. Somehow, they descended to Unuyi, at 10,000 feet, where Ben searched high and low for help. Fortunately, he speaks fluent Spanish and had the wherewithal to find a Jeep owner who would drive them.

In Bolivia, getting to lower elevation presents a problem. A glance at the globe shows a broad crest of mountains occupying the country's western half. Ben had told me they would be traveling across the mountains to Sucre, a good-sized city with a hospital. When he called me back, he said at one point the bottled oxygen stopped and Caleb passed out. Ben managed to get it flowing again.

Sucre is between 8,000 and 9,000 feet, hardly "low," but Ben was reassured by the medical care. Caleb would have to spend four days in the hospital, on antibiotics to protect against pneumonia. Pulmonary edema, in which the lungs fill with fluid, is one of several kinds of mountain sickness and is a life-threatening condition that one can't prevent ahead of time. I was impressed by the concise information and directions for treatment in the little book on mountaineering medicine from the Mountaineers in Seattle.

Ben called us at the end of an anxious day and gave me the number of a call center that would close soon. When I got back to him, he explained that his MCI card wasn't doing him much good. He lapsed into a tension-venting description of the backwardness of Bolivia, and yet we both know competent and caring Bolivians lent a hand to help them. In circumstances like this, a facility in Spanish and a cool head go a long way. I was weak in both areas. I failed to coordinate a call between Ben and Caleb's parents, who had to get their information second-hand for awhile.

It's been a trying week in Lake Woebegone—or North of Ned, as the case may be. It's time for those who have been in danger to get well. The two young men are learning to negotiate a wide world that can be dangerous, a world that can take you by surprise. The underlying message is to prepare for the difficult times as well as to reach out for the ambitious dream. Our children are learning, and we learn—always—from them.

—July 10, 1997

He walked up to the house bare-foot, when the light and shade had a summer cast and the pine woods smelled entirely different than they do in winter.

Remembering another graduation

When I look forward to the pomp and circumstance of graduation ceremonies scheduled this weekend, another graduation comes to mind. While so many will be gazing proudly at their robe-draped sons and daughters and being reminded by speakers of the great significance of the occasion, I might give myself a moment to savor the memory of that graduation four or five summers past.

It was a mid-summer's day and I hadn't seen my oldest son for months. I'd gotten used to his traveling, in a way, and to his being out of communication for fairly long periods. I'd learned a kind of negative approach to worry: no news is, for the moment, good news.

I'm talking about a kid who dropped out of high school in the tenth grade. I think it was definitely his choice to do so. I remember a lot of adults thrashing over their responsibilities in the matter and coming up with a variety of explanations why this incredibly bright young man had turned away from the education establishment. We all looked kind of foolish, trying to close the barn door after the horse had fled.

I look back and see many good intentioned teachers, some flip-flopping administrators, and most of all a pair of very inexperienced young parents who had brought a child into the world before they'd fully grown up themselves, and who hadn't the skill to guide him through the confusions of divorce and a radically changing world. When fate dealt the cards, he didn't get the same support many of the satin-garbed graduates did, though many of them made do with less.

I'm not saying that anyone failed where my son was concerned. In fact, that is why I relish so much the memory of him showing up unannounced that summer day. He walked up to the house barefoot, when the light and shade had a summer cast and the pine woods smelled entirely different than they do in winter. His clothes were ragged and his dark curls cascaded over his brow. His smile eclipsed the sun. His presence, unembellished, often feels like a gift to me, and that quality overrides the sophistication of a diploma. But on that day, in his hand, he had a record of his GED (General Equivalency Diploma), passed with flying colors.

What could I say, how could I toast him? I made a pot of coffee, opened a can of milk, piled a plate with cinnamon toast and scrambled some fresh eggs a neighbor had given me. I sat down with him at the table and beamed. I don't think any formal fanfare could compare with the satisfaction of that visit.

There were problems still; that I could see. And I think many parents of this weekend's graduates will feel the same way—how incomplete the process thus far. But the graduation I'm talking about was mine, not his. I graduated into a new faith in my son, knowing he would do things in his own space and own time, defiant at times of the forms of society. I knew the will to succeed and to survive was in him.

—June 2, 1988

Books
of all sorts
were her
field guides
to the
human
race...

She skinny dipped in the ocean of light

P hotographer Laura Gilpin expressed a common sentiment when she wrote that work is what carried you through the difficult times. And it is time for me to get back to work; put pen to paper; let my mind weave words and surprise me with its fabric. Writing is a process with its own life: you write not what others want to hear, not necessarily what you thought you ought. Rather, you release what you have to give.

Since I committed last week's column on family into the care of the newspaper office computer, I have held my mother's hand and basked in the sunshine of her smile for the last time. Now memories will have to serve, and thank goodness there are many.

I am awed by the outpouring from my mother's friends that was as extravagant at the beginning of her illness as it was years later at its end. Offerings of flowers, food and books never faltered. Books! The more she was limited to her bed, the more the nearby table groaned under the weight of piles of mystery and biography, best selling fiction, essay and history. Books of all sorts were her field guides to the human race, though what they had to say never exceeded the authority of her own experience.

My mother's sense of humor has saved me many times in the past week, when the atmosphere has become funereal. She didn't say funny things, but she

221

always appreciated a good joke, no matter how irreverent, as long as it rang true and shattered pretenses.

She had a dining room that she had insisted be added to the family home, a dining room wrapped with windows that looked out on Flagstaff, the Flatirons and the foothills receding northward capped by eloquent ribbons of clouds. From the dining room one could see the foothills greening or the flame of sumac in the fall, or the gorgeous lace of new snowfall on pink sandstone.

But her pleasure was the parade up and down the street and sidewalk. There was one woman who took her daily walk along this route and for some reason or another always looked as if she were pondering a cruel betrayal. "She doesn't look very happy, does she?" my mother would invariably ask. And I would take her to task for judging solely on appearances.

She sat in gentle judgment at every meal—on the dogs, the children, the young bicyclists and joggers, the older pedestrians who passed up and down the street. This was the only time she wasn't immersed in a more profound and personal attention to life.

My mother was one of many women so enthused with what the world had to offer that prejudices of gender were no barrier to her. Though she met setbacks at times because she was a woman, she accepted them in a positive way, never crippled by bitterness, simply enriched in her knowledge of the reality of her times. She loved her motherly claim on her family and the romantic renewals that came periodically in 50 years of marriage. She also had the clear intellect we too often associate with the males of our species, and it demanded constant satisfaction as well.

Predictably, the Boulder paper didn't get her obituary quite right. But that is a futile place to try to defend or define a life. My column may be no more satisfactory a slot. Last week near her bed was a pamphlet with a quote on the cover: "To be a peacemaker is to be the most radical witness to life"—she was. Pinned to the lampshade was a button declaring: "I skinny dip in the ocean of light"—she did.

—*February 5, 1987*

*Words were
important
to her, not
because
she was a
pundit but
because she
valued com-
munication
between
people.*

Belated Mother's Day greetings

My mother won't be reading this. She died of cancer a little over seven years ago. She was very weak for a long time before her death, but I still feel she was, at 73, in her prime. She was clear mentally and her eyesight had been restored by cataract surgery. Judging a lifetime, it's hard to say when is the "right" time to go, but we're rarely asked politely coming and going, so what can I say?

Lately, I've been wishing I could write to her—or wishing I'd get a letter from her. We exchanged letters when we traveled and wrote almost as often between mountains and plains, when I didn't have a phone. Letters could be a medium for sharing feelings. The doubts, the queries, the enthusiasms for things that become stilted out there in the open air—all slipped easily into observations and reports of our lives. I'd love to write to her about my grandson, though I would have to confess that I never understood how much my children meant to her.

Sometimes, I wish I could assign people a stint under her sharp grammatical ear. She used words with the care of an artist and never let go by my own sloppy approximations. She passed on to me Fowler's *Modern English Usage* and *Concise Oxford Dictionary,* instead of pieces of jewelry, and I value them highly.

I confessed recently to a friend that I didn't show her any of my published writing for years, thinking she would find fault with it. She was (by letter) wonderfully encouraging when I finally sent her a sheath of columns. But I also remember her reading a draft for me and picking out a word, holding it up like she was pinning it on the clothesline, where we could both see it clashed with my purpose.

Words were important to her, not because she was a pundit but because she valued communication between people. Her appreciation of the world was complex. Passing on her love of literature to me, she showed me that complexity and simplicity were two sides of the same coin. The simplest truths came to life in her collections of Shakespeare, Shaw, Dickens and other books shelved in the hall outside my bedroom door. She coaxed me along innumerable mountain trails or simply to the library on city sidewalks, teaching me to trust my own eyes and feet.

She was a liberal Democrat, a great participator in public affairs. Democracy was more than majority vote; the rights and feelings of each individual—deep, basic, personal needs—were part of the justice the system was designed to deliver, and grammar was part of the way that people made their points. Literature was essential training to the political mind.

She received her Ph.D. from the political science department at the University of Colorado in the 1950s—a rare feat for a woman with children in those days. As she came to the stage in cap and gown, we brats, who had done our best to obstruct her intellectual pursuits, stood up and cheered.

I feel my distance from her now, at the same time I know her "who's" and "whom's" are imbedded in me forever, along with many more intangible rules of life. A certain processing goes on after death: who was she? who was I to her? what truly signified in our relationship? what pains and joys did we inflict on one another? My questioning has been resolved, the ambiguous answers filed and accepted. I remain, missing her, grateful at my best to be a vessel of her critical and appreciative approach to life.

—*May 12, 1994*

*The hard-
wood trees
in town,
imported
for land-
scaping,
reminded
me of pets...*

With Boo on my back

In my notes to myself I find this, applicable any week of the year: "Write a column. Unfortunately, this is a command, not an idea."

This week's column-writing agonies have included the production of a ponderous, convoluted commentary on "family values." I'm going to junk it and give you instead more notes from my journal:

My grandson, the pack and I are very happy together. I took him for a walk last week across Boulder. I was hardly out the door with him than I was struck by his quiet awareness and flooded with gratitude to be able to look at the familiar land with him, traversing routes I've walked for decades. From a high spot near Casey Junior High, I looked out on the curves and crevasses around the Flatirons and searched out the seeps tangled with shrubs, dormant with wild iris, where I played as a child. Then I turned to the north and admired that line between plains and foothills, diminishing like a perspective line running to infinity.

I talked to the kid behind me to stay in touch: "How's it going, Boo? Nice, huh?" But what was so satisfying about walking with him was that I didn't need to speak my thoughts to him. He's got eyes to see it, and he settled into a reverence, a reverie, as he rocked to my striding motion over the built-up bluffs, across the river valley.

A woman stopped to let us cross an empty street and rolled down the window to inquire if I would come to the courthouse lawn the next day with the baby for a picture, celebrating the year of the family. I can't, I explained. I'm only with him one day a week. We're going to see his great-grandfather today. Oh, she shook her head wistfully—that'd be great. It's okay, I consoled her, you'll have lots of wonderful people there, I'm sure.

But was there anything so wonderful as Boo, sound asleep against my back, absorbing into his dreams the shallow sounds of the winter creek, until we slipped inside his great-grandfather's door. There he woke to a strange place but was immediately reassured by the old folks' faces. He smiled at them the way he smiles at a cat, pleased to have found such satisfactory life-forms in this universe. He loved the dancing patterns of fabrics, collected from all over the world, and the walls of books that line their living room. Set down on the floor, he raised his head, his back arched high, or he sat in my lap, struggling to bring an empty mug to his mouth; he is at a stage where everything is to be grasped and mouthed.

He was awake, silent and serious behind me, all the way home, and I was sure the sounds of water slipping over rocks and of ravens cawing from tall trees were an integral part of his day—besides the traffic grit and grime, the city furtiveness and the copious tufts of litter that contradict all myths connecting growth with progress.

We stopped in the library, where the bookshelves and windowsills were lined with pots of lanky narcissus in bloom—their oniony scent somewhere between sweet and rank. I bent to one and kept it to myself, wondering if a hint of its fragrance had entered his day, realizing with a jolt that it really was January, and the days were growing longer.

The hardwood trees in town, imported for landscaping, reminded me of pets—except for the cottonwoods and crab apples which are more likely to belong here. Town trees are domesticated, exotic but thriving. Their shapes are years in the making, pruned like poodle clips, but with graceful, wild genes directing growth patterns of their own: oak, maple, elm, catalpa, honey locust. Looking at them, with Boo on my back, they were all within my grasp in a special way I do not have alone.

—January 27, 1994

The driver cheered young Superman as he made a great, successful, two-footed leap from bus step to sidewalk.

Grandmas and superheros

For the past year or two, I have picked up my grandson at his day care center on Thursdays, and we have walked or ridden the bus back to his home. This time away from a dependence on the automobile has a precious quality for both of us. I no longer push the stroller for him. Now, he has two marvelously strong legs and a bold, congratulatory stride.

When I arrive at the Children's Center to pick him up, the other children greet me pleasantly. "Billy, your granma's here!" they'll shout, or just inform me, "He's over there." Sometimes they'll sidle up to me, eyes round and eager. "I'd like to go to your house," they'll say, or "I wish I could go on the bus with you." I've gotten to know these kids, learning their names before they could talk, and now, well, they can talk—my grandson being something of a champion at it.

Last Thursday, I passed through a dark and quiet classroom to the playground drenched in afternoon sun and buzzing frenetically with children at play. Billy was galloping back and forth at the head of a small band of super heroes. He had on his Superman top—cobalt blue with a red and yellow "S" centered on his small chest, a red nylon cape pinned to his shoulder. I settled in to wait for him.

One of the luxuries of being granma is not having to scrape a clinging kid off at day care in the morning and then, alternately, drag him away from play in the after-

227

noon. I waited and watched the teachers shifting their attention from one tearful child to another, lifting, comforting, repairing, then joining in on games or instructing the 3-year-olds on social interactions.

Finally, my Superman was ready to head for home. On the first bus, he streaked to the back, choosing from some inner compass, where we joined ranks with teenagers, who consider it their private domain. Once, he sat down next to a tattooed adolescent wearing leather bristling blatant metal spikes and drooping chains. I watched Billy silently take in this punk rock warrior.

The first bus delivered us to the transit station. On our second bus, we rode closer to the front so the driver could see Billy getting off the bus and not begin to drive away while he was still negotiating the front steps (as once happened to my small son, Ben). We were riding through the car-clogged streets, with Billy intently scrutinizing the scenery, when I heard him gasp.

"Look, granma—there's Super Girl. She's just like me!" I looked out the window to see a small girl seated in a brown chair at a table in the Boulderado Hotel. In her bright blue and red costume she was as clear and dazzling as Wonder Woman on a cereal box. She had fair skin and auburn hair like little Billy's. Then, the bus swung into a curve and she was lost from view. We were stunned; it was like the moment in Dr. Zhivago when Yuri sees his lost love, Lara, from a crowded Moscow bus. We rode silently and seriously to our stop in north Boulder.

The driver cheered young Superman as he made a great, successful, two-footed leap from bus step to sidewalk. From my pack I fished out a quarter for the overpriced gum machine with the spiraling clear-plastic delivery chute. Billy clutched the coin as we made our way to the market. After shopping we headed home holding hands. When we got to the sidewalk where he could safely be on his own, I shifted the grocery bags. He took one from me. "I'll help you carry the groceries home," he insisted. And he did.

—March 20, 1997

WALKING

Liz and her grandson Boo walking in the woods.

A Life at Treeline:

WALKING

I walk as much for my own sanity as for the environment, and I walk to digest major events.

I pray with my feet.

—August 1993

The sky is like an up-turned plate—a big platter of openness heaped with thoughts.

Walking nurtures an open mind

I hope you are taking time to be wooed by the season. Snow or no snow in the air, the shortened days and clear, starry nights deserve respect. I get the feeling that this time is for learning as much as it is for giving and receiving. Maybe the best gifts come from nature, not stores.

We're having an open winter—so open, you could call it drought. The snow around my house stays clean, though. It has gone through innumerable changes and refurbishing from wind, warm spells, cold plunges, and downslope flurries—puffs of snow blow over the Divide that sometimes don't make it east of the Peak to Peak Highway. I can march through the biggest drifts in my Redwing boots, without worrying about getting wet.

The skimpy snowpack changes from day to day, week to week, so that it keeps taking a print. I can read the movements of grouse, elk, coyote, fox, bobcat, weasel, cottontail rabbit, snowshoe hare, and the ever-present, ever-busy pine squirrel. Old prints fill with dry debris. New footprints punch through the slightly hardened surface. In places, my feet crunch through a glaze of ice.

Much as I love to ski—and usually, it's the only way to travel around my house by December—nothing compares with walking for nurturing the open mind. I don't know why that is so, but I am sure it is true and that anyone who loves to walk would agree with me. An open mind doesn't mean a lack of conviction, by the way. You can believe in things deeply and still have an open mind. What counts is the seeing.

Leaving the house on foot I have an almost infinite number of choices about where I will go. One day I am called up to the "big trees" to listen to the wind. It makes a special sound defined by the shape of the hillside and the tall trunks and their wide spacing. Even the way the sun cuts through has a voice, a rhythm of shadows over modestly curved rolls of snow.

Another day I walk out the Gold Hill road. My reasoning for traveling east might be harder to define. My pleasure is in the following the views to the south, stretching out to the plains, over to Mount Evans, back to James Peak.

I am collecting a notation or translation, still rudimentary, for what I call the mountain language—the way the hills and distances and summits seem to speak as I travel and change places in perspective to where they are. Walking east on the Gold Hill Road, the foothills are like splashing waves: they slap and roll, purple to the eye. The sky is like an up-turned plate—a big platter of openness heaped with thoughts. Coming back I spot a dark bird sailing steadily towards me. It crosses above the road without a wing beat, near enough for me to feel sure it is an eagle.

Looking for it over the next rise I see the big, dark bird harried by a raven, half its size, and then another eagle soaring, white tail and head cast pure silver by the sun.

In town, the lack of snowpack and the open ground means that fierce gusts of wind stir up biting clouds of grit and dust. Outside town, an open winter means that all the hammered roads into National Forest continue to invite marauders. The roadside environment knows no rest. The abuses, the man-made deserts scuffed bare by tires, look desiccated and sad. Plentiful snow not only closes off some country, but gives the impression of healing the land.

I think that walking opens me up to place and I would recommend it to anyone. If you live in town, walk at least to its edge, and better yet, beyond it. Experiment with the in and out of where your feet will take you. Bring this season, time and place home with you.

—December 15, 1994

Call the cops, this tundra's been murdered by a gang of all-terrain vehicles!

Mountains are sometimes victims

I have always had a need to hike alone, at least some of the time. I like to take off without too much planning and leave the house behind, with its familiar routines hanging from it like so many lead fishing weights.

As a friend puts it, when you hike alone you can blow your nose when you feel like it, without saying excuse me. You can let your thoughts go where they want to go. You can be silently fascinated by things as simple as tree bark, as complex as a camouflaged fawn or a black swallowtail beating against a stiff wind on the tundra.

I don't always know where I'm going when I leave to hike alone. North, south, east, west—something inside me reacts like a needle in a compass; a certain view, a certain mood to the landscape, or the idea of seeing a particular bird or flower pulls me one way or another.

These impromptu flights from home are always rewarded by unpredictable treasures, such as the sight of two does walking with enviable relaxation away from a pond, a hawk rising from the top of a nearby tree or an eagle flapping up from a valley below me. Sometimes I see a bird or a flower I have never seen before, or a meadow of wildflowers neither one day short of nor past its full glory. These things present themselves as gifts.

Then, there is another kind of surprise. I think people often don't walk alone because they distrust the woods and meadows. I used to have an unreasonable suspicion I'd come across a body, a human corpse, in the woods. That's been happening with uncomfortable regularity in our mountains, but it hasn't happened to me.

Instead, I come across scenes of death and destruction of another kind, and they are all the more demoralizing because there's no one to go to and say: Help! I just found a mutilated tree! Or, Call the cops, this tundra's been murdered by a gang of all-terrain vehicles!

This summer the destruction is pressing closer and closer to home. A lovely valley I used to visit often was marred by a camper of such violent tendencies my stomach was turned when I came upon the scene. Aspen trees were plastered with shot and savagely hacked with an ax. Saplings lay severed on the ground, and, in the middle of it all, trash overran a huge blackened fire ring.

Even the tundra of the United Nations Biosphere on Niwot Ridge has been violated by off-road vehicles this year. And I have been hiding from my sense of loss, foot dragging when I ought to be walking.

My experience is far from unique. Population pressures are intensifying on our mountains, and such a kind of violent release from the city is scarring them each summer day. We do have land management agencies to report to, however, and we must let them know how much we care with phone calls and letters. The land has always been an enduring thing, we might tell them, but the pressures are so intense, that given eyes to see, we worry for its survival.

—*July 23, 1987*

In your softest shoes, step off the trail, massage the land with your feet and let the land massage you.

Discovering the surface of the land

My youngest son, Dan, takes one look at my ideas in their raw form and gives a skeptical shrug. "Yeah, but...," he responds, forcing me to grab hold of something in particular and pin it down for him. I tried out my idea of "surface" as an environmental concept on him over the phone the other night.

"That's pretty deep, Mom," he snickered.

It's true, the idea of the surface of the land as something significant is deep to a society that mines for gold and paves for gamblers and gawkers. For those to whom the scenery is inanimate, a hill an invitation for a cut, wild grass a waste of space and trees a harvest for a lumber company, surface goes deep.

Even when the land is buried under snow, though, we can approach the concept. After a snowfall, before the plows and path-beating footfalls of our busy lives transform it, we witness an integrity that is inherently pleasing and that functions for many living things.

Growing up at the edge of an expanding western town gave me an appreciation of surface. I was often stepping from paved streets onto something else. There, the earth would be lumpy, bumpy, swampy, scratchy, rocky, muddy, sometimes hard and sometimes soft under my feet; I loved it.

Now I cringe when I see a child digging up moss with the toe of his shoe. I feel the weight of a big truck hurtling across a hill. I blush at the crudity of mountain

237

bikers who spin their wheels against an island of grass. In each case, the surface is being violated, and though we don't ordinarily recognize its importance, being sensitive to it is part of environmental awareness.

Snow is part of the surface, caught and patterned by forests and grasses. We can visualize the surface of the land as patterned by loft and nap to hold moisture and moderate wind and air temperatures. The fallen needles of the lodgepole forest form a soil-trapping felt that is easily broken up by heavy travel. Fallen trunks in the forest create another layer: a lattice work that slowly decomposes into moss-green exhalations as brilliant as emeralds.

Depressions in the mountain landscape become fertile sloughs. Wet for half the summer, they dry each year into a crust as crunchy as french bread. Above timberline the surface is magical. Lichen-covered, frost-heaved rocks create fissures that seem to lead to another world, and the cushioning clumps of vegetation are colored by the pigments of different species. Snow drifts to the lee of the slightest bumps, insulating some plants and assuring their survival. Now, the willows and krummholz evergreens just below the tundra are already several feet deep in snow.

The surface of the land is an incredibly engineered solar collector. In turn, it produces all that we human beings depend on: plants that produce oxygen, plants and animals that provide food and medicine, roots and leaves that filter air and water.

To become more aware of this "deep" concept of surface, try parking your car for a day or two a week. Even if you walk on pavement, you will notice more of the fabric of the land. Read *Brooks Range Passage,* by David Cooper, an account of a month-long walk across an Alaskan wilderness. In your softest shoes, step off the trail, massage the land with your feet and let the land massage you. Listen to the wind running through trees and grasses; touch the raw edges of highway cuts. Am I making sense, Dan?

—*November 7, 1991*

Give gift
of walking shoes

I remember a day like today, when the nice weather held, the snow had been polished to a crust and the roads were scoured bare. My two younger sons and I had spent the day walking and came indoors to discover that only one kerosene lamp still had fuel in it. We passed the evening sitting around that burning edge of cotton wick, with our reading, games and drawing, while the starlight flickered in the windows and the hulk of Mt. Audubon was outlined against the sky.

It was the Solstice, and burning the last of our kerosene seemed an appropriate symbol of the season. The evening was in keeping with the day and our slow moving agenda. Our walks, in which we became a part of the living planet in a very ordinary way, came about when the weight of being inside was too heavy to bear. The boys would find what they were going to wear and if there was anything special they wanted to take: the right hat or mittens, a stick or compass. These things were important, plus a snack and water. Then we would go outside and set an objective, or just a direction.

Sometimes I made my kids walk with me over great distances in bitter cold. I'd be gentler to them now, I know, but I tried to reward them: "Catch up, Mustard," I cajoled. We played word games and did math puzzles in our heads: addition, multiplication, fractions. We told tales with our own variations on Jack in the Beanstalk or "The Mountain Goats of Temlahan."

As we walked, talked and grumbled, we worked our way in through a portal—something like C.S. Lewis' wardrobe full of coats—to a place of awe and simple competence, on foot, outdoors. The passage is scratchy and obstructive at times. I still have to coax myself to get there. I used to do it for them, bribing and threatening, talking and telling, adjusting their clothes, warming them and resting them, then starting over, explaining the simple necessity of reaching a destination.

Suddenly, they'd be leading me into the most innocent awareness of what lay about us: the color of the vegetation, of water and sky, the clouds and mountains shaped fantastically, the tracks in the snow and bird flight above us, as well as their ideas, percolating up from a subterranean store of possibilities. I could play, too, and answer them freely.

Walking with children has many practical sides to it. Along the way, my children learned the safe places in the road and to react to the sounds of traffic, as well as short cuts or digressions through the woods. As we walked as a family, Skip added the challenge of side-stepping steep, loose slopes without sending a single rock crashing down. He fed their love of competition or towed them behind him on a thin rope to keep them climbing the steep sides of Niwot Ridge.

When they went out on their own, they knew to take proper clothes and leave notes about where they were going—notes I still find stuck in books naming places found on no maps, only in our communal experience—Panther Rock, Columbine Valley, Benji's Trough; notes describing the routes they would take and when they expected to return. They learned to wrap extra mittens around Nalgene bottles of hot tea on solo skis, to wear bike helmets and bright clothing when traveling on two wheels. They learned basic safety procedures and something else. When they'd come home, we'd trace their routes on topo maps, discuss their mileage—where are you, who are you, how far can you go and what do you see?

Walking with children does them a favor, teaching them to use the first gifts they were given.

—*December 16, 1993*

> *Now, I can't walk and I miss it, but it is not cause for remorse. One feels remorse for the things one could have done and didn't.*

Walking has been the nicest thing

I t seemed like the most natural thing to take for granted, that I would always be able to walk. All my life I have loved to walk and given half a chance would spend my time walking, over and above any other activity. Now, for reasons still mysterious to myself and the medical establishment, my feet will hardly bear me across the street.

I try to reflect intelligently on this situation. I'm glad I covered so much territory while I could. I'm grateful, in a reserved sort of way, for a perspective from the other side of the fence. I called RTD the other day to see if I could use public transportation for a doctor's appointment. When I found the bus was four blocks short of my destination, I had to say, "No way, José, gotta drive." I'm learning what it would take to make a truly functional public transportation system, not one that serves only the athletically capable.

Nowadays, when I can get to my car, I get a charge out of pressing the accelerator—I used to think this was a sign of poor character. I love the empowerment of being able to go somewhere, not dependent on my own steam. It used to be the other way around. While it is a pleasure to cruise the open highway, however, the pleasure is mundane. On a morning like today, I recall setting out on foot in a quiet, snow-swept landscape warming under the rays of the sun—the pleasure was incomparable, celestial, spiritual.

Looking back on my walking history, I recall only as murky background having to keep up with my parents in town and in the mountains. I remember with more clarity my own enthusiastic embrace of fall mornings, when I would wake at dawn to new snow and slip out of the house to be the first to put my footprints on the land, except for the four-legged critters who had left their impressions around the wet stain of the creek in the undeveloped lands to the west.

As a pre-teen and teenager, my friend and I explored Boulder streets and surrounding open spaces on foot. We would go for "penny hikes" in the Hill area, tossing a coin at every intersection to determine our route (this time of year, scuffing our feet through fallen leaves). I took bets in the cafeteria of Baseline Junior High on whether or not I could walk across town from my piano lessons in under 45 minutes. I could and I won a pot of nickels.

I was a fast walker on the trail and an intrepid explorer off the trail. I had enough training from the Colorado Mountain Club and my mountaineering father to feel safe by myself, wherever I might end up. It was something of a shock, after bringing three children into the world, to discover I wasn't as fleet of foot as I used to be. By the time the youngest started cajoling me up the trails behind him, I was more amused than chagrined by this juxtaposition of roles.

Now, I can look to summits along the Divide and recall how they felt underfoot and what the view is like from them. I'm proudest of Navajo—a long haul, a creep over steep ridges and a shimmy up a chimney to the top of its tilted cone. I'm most familiar with Audubon—which I've hiked dozens of times in approximately 45 years. I'm fondest of James Peak—that is probably a story in itself. I've explored gulches and hillsides that see little human traffic. When I see them from the highway, I know what lives and grows there and how it feels to be there at different times of the year, different times of day.

Walking was the ultimate freedom. I could take myself anywhere I wanted to go, one easy step at a time. With joints and muscles naturally aligned, it was as smooth as flight, an unquestionable gift, an easily guarded right. I felt like I fit on the landscape; with my feet I traced maps inside myself. Now, I can't walk and I miss it, but it is not cause for remorse. One feels remorse for the things one could have done and didn't.

—November 6, 1997